Scotland and the Arts

Wherever you go in Scotland, you are confronted with evidence of the richness and vibrancy of Scotland's culture. From the poetry of Douglas Dunn, Sorley Maclean, Liz Lochhead and Edwin Morgan to the novels of Janice Galloway, Irvine Welsh, Alasdair Gray and James Kelman, writing in Scotland is as strong as in the days of Burns and MacDiarmid. Paintings by Alison Watt, Elizabeth Blackadder, Steven Campbell and John Bellany together with sculpture by Eduardo Paolozzi and Ian Hamilton Finlay grace galleries in these artists' home country as well as throughout the world. Conceptual artists such as Tracy Mackenna, Christine Borland, Douglas Gordon, Louise Scullion and Matthew Dalziel are establishing a world-wide reputation.

Performing arts range from an all woman drumming group through to major orchestras such as the Royal Scottish National Orchestra, the Scottish Chamber Orchestra and the BBC Scottish Symphony Orchestra and jazz players of the calibre of Tommy Smith and Steven Hamilton. Composers such as James MacMillan, Sir Peter Maxwell Davies and Sally Beamish are presenting contemporary classical music to a range of audiences in Scotland and internationally. Opera and ballet are performed in a variety of venues, from large venues such as the Edinburgh Festival Theatre, the Theatre Royal in Glasgow and His Majesty's Theatre in Aberdeen to small arts centres like the MacRobert in Stirling. Performance art based groups present work at the cutting edge of visual theatre and new plays by Scottish writers such as David Greig, Sue Glover and Ian Heggie are presented by a range of exciting and dynamic theatre companies at the Tron, the Traverse and by touring companies such as Communicado. Performances take place in theatres, schools, community centres, converted factories and in the many festivals that take place throughout Scotland during the year.

The shortlisting of Edinburgh and the subsequent award to Glasgow of City of Architecture and Design 1999 is testimony to the work of contemporary artists working in these important areas. In crafts also, Scots lead the way in producing jewellery, textiles and glass that are exported throughout the world, and crafts people such as Peter Chang are winning prizes for Scotland.

Traditional music, too, has never been in such demand. The Celtic Connections Festival has found audiences in excess of 80,000 for a two week festival in January which offers workshops, lectures and performances. Balnain House in Inverness has established a strong reputation for offering an unrivalled series of concerts, workshops and classes in all that the best of Scottish traditional music has to offer, including the making of the instruments. The Royal Scottish Academy of Music and Drama now offers courses in traditional music as part of that college's mainstream curriculum.

In 1762, at the height of the period known as the Scottish Enlightenment, Voltaire, the French philosopher and writer wrote "It is from Scotland that we receive rules of taste in all the arts." Some would say that Scotland is in a second period of enlightenment, but whatever your interest, there is no doubt that contemporary Scotland can offer a range of artists and initiatives which display the excitement of being in Scotland at a time when national identity is high on the agenda and when the issue of Scotland's relationship with the rest of the international community is actively being explored at a political, social and cultural level.

This guide is a structural look at the arts in Scotland and offers a brief description of some of the main arts organisations that help to create the culture of the country that is Scotland.

The following pages show a small selection of the arts in Scotland
1 Royal Scottish National Orchestra
2 Aly Bain and the BT Scottish Ensemble
3 'Sharp Shorts', Traverse Theatre
4 'Turandot', Scottish Opera
5 Scottish Ballet
6 Scottish Dance Theatre
7 Scottish Literature
8 Aberdeen Art Gallery
9 Keiko Mukaide
10 'Sargassum', Dalziel and Scullion
11 'Born under a Cloud', Steven Campbell
12 'European Bison', Sally Matthews, Tyrebagger Sculpture Project
13 Quality Scottish films, 'Trainspotting', 'Braveheart', 'Fridge', 'Good Day for the Bad Guys', 'An Lobaist' (The Sacrifice), 'Shallow Grave', 'Small Faces', 'Roimh Ghaoth A' Gheamhraidh' (Before Winter Winds), 'Franz Kafka's It's a Wonderful Life',
14 'Beauty and the Beast', Edinburgh Puppet Company
15 'At the Edge of the Meadow', Wendy McMurdo (1996)

Nam Bitheadh Agams' Eilean

Nam bitheadh agams' eilean
Is caisteal beag na chois
Le caoraich agus croitearan
Is *poll tax* duine bochd
Is làn nan cnoc de chearcan-fraoich
Is fèidh tha math 'son spòrs
Bòtannan uaine
Fore-and-aft
Geansaidh le tuill
Is fuaimreagan cruinn

Nam bitheadh agams' eilean
Is plèana beag dhomh fhin
Le *Range Rover* shìos a' feitheamh
Airson mo chrògan mìn
Is sgalagan de gheamairean
A' gogadaich mu m'shàil
Leas làn lusan
Le feansaichean àrd'
Geataichean glaiste
Is soighnichean dearg

Chan fhuirinn-s' ann a bharrachd,

'hionn 's Gu Robh Mi Measail Air

...uaraich
...is
...'chràdhadh

...d 's mo thoileachas
... do chor
...adar
...igeil às

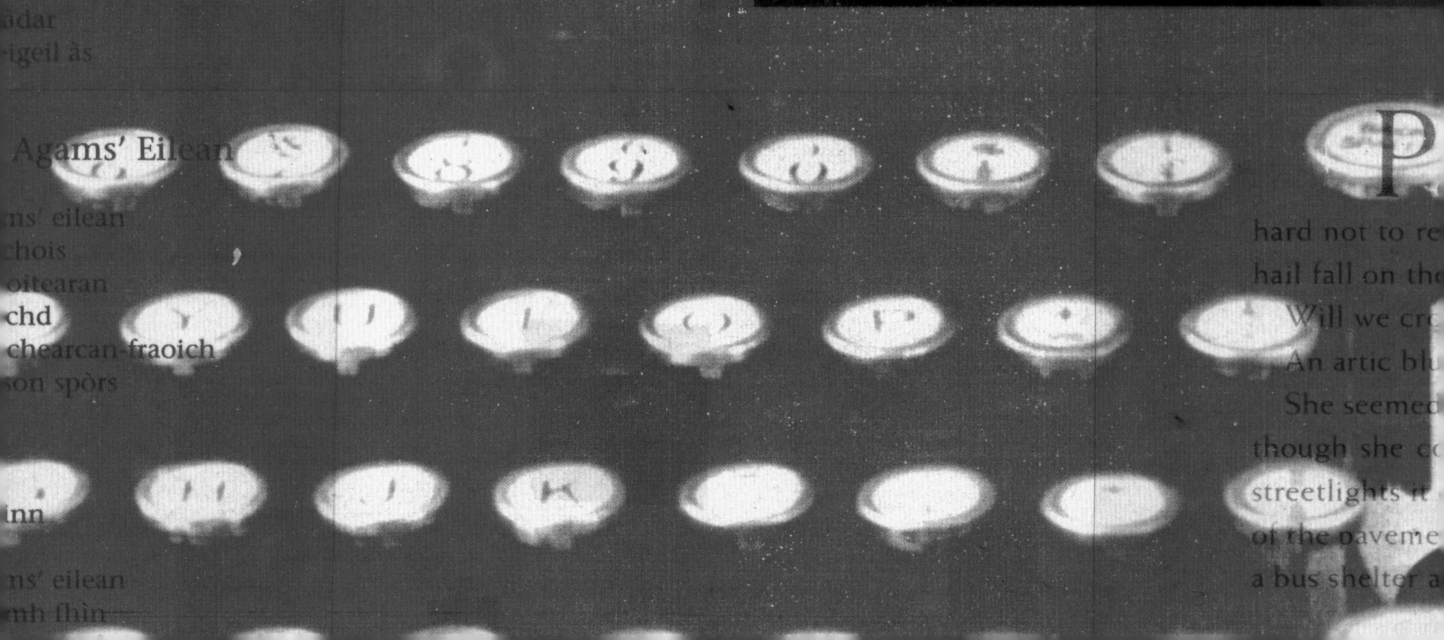

Agams' Eilean

...ns' eilean
...chois
...oitearan
...chd
...chearcan-fraoich
...son spòrs

...inn

...ns' eilean
...mh fhin

hard not to re...
hail fall on the...
Will we cr...
An artic blu...
She seemed...
though she c...
streetlights ...
of the paveme...
a bus shelter a...

17

Scotland

Scotland is a country of some 30,414 square miles (78,772 square kilometres) including some 609 square miles of freshwater lochs, and has a population of around 5 million. It is a third of the land mass of Great Britain, with 9% of its population. The largest city, Glasgow, has a population density of 3,428 people per square kilometre, whilst Sutherland, at the northern end of the country has 3 people per square kilometre. The Highland region is the size of Belgium and has a population of only 200,000.

As well as the mainland, Scotland has some 790 islands, ranging from large rocks to land which is several hundred square miles in area. Of these, the largest and best known are the groups of Shetland and Orkney in the north-east; Lewis, Harris, Mull, Skye and Islay in the Hebrides - the string of islands which lies off the west coast of Scotland - and the islands of Bute and Arran in the Firth of Clyde. Approximately 130 of the Scottish islands are inhabited.

Scotland is a nation but not a state. It is part of the United Kingdom of Great Britain and Northern Ireland. The Union of the Crowns in 1603 and the Union of Parliaments in 1707 removed Scotland's statehood but did not remove its sense of being a distinct nation with a distinct cultural identity. Under the terms of the Act of Union in 1707 and other measures, it retains autonomy in judicial, ecclesiastical and educational matters.

Culturally, Scotland has developed independently of the rest of the UK, although there is considerable interchange with many countries, particularly through the major international festivals.

Three main languages are spoken in Scotland: Scots (with a number of variants such as Doric which is spoken in the north-east), Gaelic, spoken by some 80,000 Scots mostly in the Islands and down the west coast, and English. Each has a range of cultural activities associated with it which is reflected in these pages.

18

Government and the Arts

Scotland's arts are supported through a combination of sources: Government funding, channelled through the Scottish Office to the main funding agencies such as the Scottish Arts Council and the Scottish Film Council; the National Lottery, established by Government to provide additional support for good causes; local authorities who contribute substantially to the provision of museums, theatres, galleries, libraries and teachers of arts subjects; commercial and trade union sponsorship of specific arts events and organisations; and earned income. Public sector support for the arts is achieved in a number of ways.

THE SCOTTISH OFFICE

The Scottish Office is the Government department responsible for the administration of legislation specific to Scotland, for Scotland's institutions and for that portion of the Treasury budget which Government decides is appropriate to the administration of Scotland, including to local authorities, the Scottish Education system, the arts and cultural heritage and the Scottish Courts. The Scottish Office is headed by the Secretary of State for Scotland who is a member of the Cabinet of Her Majesty's Government.

The Secretary of State for Scotland is responsible for maintaining the culture and heritage of Scotland. He is responsible for overall policy, the support structure and sponsoring legislation. The Secretary of State is financially responsible for the arts and cultural heritage structure, which is administered by the Arts and Cultural Heritage Division of the Scottish Office Education and Industry Department. The primary responsibility in this area is for the national bodies which

conserve and promote Scotland's culture. In this way, funding is allocated to the National Institutions of Scotland (the National Galleries, the National Library and the National Museums of Scotland) as well as to the Scottish Museums Council (SMC), the Scottish Arts Council (SAC) and the Scottish Film Council (SFC).

THE NATIONAL LOTTERY

The National Lottery was introduced by the Government to provide extra support for good causes which do not usually have first call on public funds. Five causes were identified by the National Lottery etc. Act 1993: the arts, including film, sports, the national heritage, charitable institutions and Millennium projects, each of which receives 20% of the net proceeds available for distribution. Lottery funds allocated to the arts in Scotland are distributed by the Scottish Arts Council.

Although SAC operates under Lottery Directions issued by the Secretary of State, decisions on applications for funding are taken by the Scottish Arts Council entirely independently

of Government. The National Heritage Memorial Fund is the distributing body for Lottery funds allocated to the national heritage throughout the UK. Based in London, it seeks advice on Lottery applications from relevant sources such as the Scottish Museums Council and Historic Scotland.

LOCAL GOVERNMENT

Local Government in Scotland is delivered by 32 unitary authorities, created by the Local Government (Scotland) Act in 1994. Prior to their coming into being in April 1996, Scotland had a two tier system of local government, based on regions and districts. Since April 1996, all the functions of local government have been provided by unitary authorities. Elections for unitary authority councillors are held every three years, and elected members deal with a wide range of services which affect the public at local level including, social services, education, housing, roads, cultural services, planning, economic development and licensing. Other services such as the police force and transport are dealt

with by joint boards comprising representatives of different authorities to allow for strategic planning and some, such as water and sewerage, are dealt with by quangos (quasi autonomous non - governmental bodies) whose representatives are appointed by the Secretary of State for Scotland.

Local authorities have placed upon them by Government a duty to provide an adequate range of arts facilities, and many local authorities are direct promoters of arts activities as well as providers of grants and facilities. Many local authorities own and manage theatres, art galleries and museums.

1

Local government is financed through direct funding from the Scottish Office and through local taxation in the form of the Council Tax, levied and collected by the local authorities.

Total local authority expenditure on the arts amounts to more than £200 million, including support for services such as galleries, museums, libraries, performing and visual arts and teachers of arts subjects. This support also includes arts related expenditure within social work and community education budgets. Local authority involvement in the arts goes well beyond providing financial support and they make a crucial contribution to arts promotion and development. The Charter for the Arts in Scotland, the widest consultation exercise on the arts in Scotland ever undertaken, confirmed the status of local authorities as "the structural pivot of cultural life in Scotland".

THE CONVENTION OF SCOTTISH LOCAL AUTHORITIES

Local government in Scotland is represented collectively by the Convention of Scottish Local Authorities (COSLA). Formed in 1975, COSLA exists to promote and protect the interests of local authorities in Scotland by providing a forum for discussion of matters of common concern. COSLA ascertains the views of member councils and communicates these to central Government, other bodies and the public. All local authorities in Scotland are members of COSLA.

The structure of COSLA provides for meetings of the full Convention, a Strategy Forum and a number of policy fora. An Education and Cultural Services policy forum addresses the cross-service issues of education, arts, sport, libraries and museums.

The Education and Cultural Services forum comments to the Scottish Office, Scottish Arts Council, Scottish Museums Council and other national bodies on issues of policy affecting local authorities in Scotland. The forum is also responsible for producing the standards for the Public Library Service in Scotland, works with the Museums and Galleries Commission in promoting the Museums Registration Scheme and, with the Scottish Arts Council, organises surveys of local authority expenditure on the arts. The successful COSLA/SALVO (Scottish Arts Lobby) conferences on the arts are also organised by the forum, jointly with SALVO. Much of this work is

undertaken by working groups comprising officer advisers and elected members.

Local authorities play a significant role in the development and funding of arts initiatives in Scotland. COSLA has close links with SAC on national and strategic arts issues and many local authorities work in partnership with SAC on local policy and projects. Individual local authorities have developed arts strategies for their areas and support local arts organisations both in cash and in kind. In addition to such local support, COSLA recommends to local authorities that they should fund the five national performing companies according to a formula devised by the Committee, and which produces over £600,000 per annum.

For more information about local government and the arts in Scotland contact:
The Convention of Scottish Local Authorities, Rosebery House, 9 Haymarket Terrace, Edinburgh EH12 5XZ
Tel: +44 131 474 9200
Fax:+44 131 474 9292

1 Grainne Morton, 'Flower Theatre' brooch   2 Siobhan Redmond and Jennifer Black in 'The Trick is to Keep Breathing', at the Tron Theatre   3 Dorothea Smartt, 'Motor Mouths', performance poetry at CCA   4 Yggdrasil Quartet

The British Council

The British Council promotes educational, cultural and technical co-operation between Britain and other countries. The Council's work, funded through the Government's Foreign and Commonwealth Office, is designed to establish long term and world-wide partnerships and to improve international understanding.

The British Council promotes educational, cultural and technical co-operation between Britain and other countries. The Council's work, funded through the Government's Foreign and Commonwealth Office, is designed to establish long term and world-wide partnerships and to improve international understanding. The Council is Britain's principal agency for cultural relations with other countries and is an integral part of the United Kingdom's overall diplomatic and aid effort. The British Council is an independent organisation incorporated by Royal Charter and registered in England as a charity. It seeks to create an understanding and appreciation of Britain and to develop partnerships by providing access to British ideas, talents and experience. The British Council is represented in 200 towns and cities in 109 countries and runs 145 libraries and 94 English teaching centres.

In promoting British arts overseas the British Council demonstrates the diversity and quality of British creative and performing artists, and fosters collaborative relationships. It provides information and advice, arranges professional exchanges and training and organises and assists

financially over 1,000 arts events a year.

Arts work in Scotland, with the creation of the first ever post of International Arts Officer based in Glasgow, has greatly raised the profile of Scottish culture overseas. The thrust of the International Arts Officer programme is to demonstrate the quality and diversity of the arts activities throughout Scotland, both in its national and international context and appeal.

British Council offices overseas co-operate with their local arts communities in a variety of ways. They may present arts events themselves, they may contribute through financial or other aid to events mounted by others, but they also offer scholarships, courses and training in Britain, support two way professional visits, and provide advice and information about the arts in Britain. In this they rely on The British Council's arts departments and officers in London and in Scotland. These departments select work for presentation abroad, giving careful thought to the local context, and provide managerial and financial support. These in turn are guided by advisory committees drawn from a broad spectrum of creative and performing artists, writers, critics, academics and administrators.

For enquiries about The British Council and its work in the arts in Scotland contact:
The International Arts Officer Scotland, The British Council, 6 Belmont Crescent, Glasgow G12 8ES
Tel: +44 141 339 8651
Fax:+44 141 337 2271
e-mail:
Rainey.Colgan@britcoun.org

VISITING ARTS

Visiting Arts promotes cultural relations by fostering the appreciation and understanding of the arts of other countries in Britain. It provides information and advice and acts as a broker between British promoters and the cultural representatives of other countries, and in relevant circumstances provides financial support. Although it is located with The British Council's Arts Division, Visiting Arts is a joint venture of the British Council, the Foreign and Commonwealth Office, the four UK Arts Councils and the Crafts Council.

For enquiries about the Visiting Arts Unit contact:
The Director, Visiting Arts, The British Council, 11 Portland Place, London W1N 4EJ
Tel: +44 171 389 3019
Fax:+44 171 389 3016

The Scottish Arts Council

The Scottish Arts Council (SAC) is one of the principal channels of Government funding for the Arts in Scotland. An autonomous organisation, responsible to and financed directly by the Scottish Office, it received £24.477 million in grant aid for 1996/7. The Scottish Arts Council was constituted under Royal Charter on 1st April 1994. Prior to this time, the Scottish Arts Council was part of the Arts Council of Great Britain (now the Arts Council of England). The Council comprises up to 16 members appointed by the Secretary of State for Scotland who are charged with setting the policies and priorities of the organisation each year, and with ensuring that decisions are taken in the interest of the Scottish public and the arts organisations that seek to serve that public.

The Scottish Arts Council aims to create a climate in which arts of quality flourish and are enjoyed by a wide range of people throughout Scotland. It does so by providing grants, advice, information, commissioning research and by working in partnership with others to develop the arts. Its policies are framed within the context of the Charter for the Arts - the result of the most extensive consultation ever undertaken on the future of the arts in Scotland- and are published each year in the Council's corporate plan.

Major arts organisations are funded by SAC on a continuing revenue basis and their work is assessed each year. In addition, SAC makes project funds available through a wide range of schemes to individual artists and arts organisations. The Council also distributes Lottery funds, available for capital projects in the arts. Guidelines for all such schemes are publicised annually. The Scottish Arts Council has a staff of about 60 people to assist in delivering these goals.

The day to day work of the Scottish Arts Council is carried out by art form departments, each of whom has a committee of specialists drawn from the relevant disciplines who advise and assist the Council in reaching a final decision on funding, policy and arts development needs.

CRAFTS

The Crafts Department promotes and supports the development of contemporary crafts including indigenous crafts throughout Scotland. The Crafts Department assists a wide range of crafts projects, education programmes and exhibitions and offers direct funding to individuals to establish themselves as makers or to develop their work.

COMBINED ARTS

The Combined Arts Department funds activities which combine literature, visual arts, crafts or film with the performing arts. This covers the work of arts centres, festivals, multi-media projects, minority ethnic arts, community arts development and service organisations for Gaelic and traditional arts, and arts and disability.

The Combined Arts Department encourages the development of community arts provision, festivals and arts centres, particularly in rural and deprived urban areas. It provides funds for experimental and innovative work created through the collaboration of artists from more than one distinct artform, and encourages the promotion of festivals dedicated to the furtherance of the Gaelic language and arts. In addition, the Department supports Gaelic arts development through a National Gaelic Arts Project

and is also interested in the development and promotion of minority ethnic arts in Scotland.

LITERATURE

The Literature Department funds a diverse range of activities to support the development of literature in Scotland. Assistance falls within three broad categories: direct aid to the writer, support for publishing and support directed towards increasing readership.

Writers with a track record of publication can receive direct help through a number of schemes including: bursaries; travel and research grants; writing fellowships; fellowships to translators and book awards.

Support is given to publishers towards the production costs of certain books and magazines; the publication costs of translated work and translators fees; literary magazines. Gaelic publishing and service organisations, such as the Scottish Publishers Association, are also funded.

SAC supports readership by funding schemes for writers in schools and in public; festivals and by providing support to organisations which promote readership.

PERFORMING ARTS

The Scottish Arts Council's Performing Arts Department encompasses Dance, Drama and Music. Each art form has its own staff and specialist advisory committee, although they work closely together to support projects involving more than one art form.

Dance

The Dance Office supports the development of dance throughout Scotland, and provides revenue support to the Scottish Ballet and to the Scottish Dance Theatre. In addition, the department gives grants and bursaries to assist with the development of new work, traditional dance and non-western dance, touring, dance artists in residence and training opportunities.

Drama

The Drama Office supports theatre, puppetry and mime throughout Scotland, and provides revenue funding both to major producing theatres and to theatre companies which tour throughout Scotland. In addition, project grants are given to assist with training, touring, the development of youth theatre and children's theatre and the encouragement of new writing by Scottish and Scottish based playwrights.

Music

The Music Office supports a wide variety of music forms including opera, orchestral and chamber music, jazz, contemporary, traditional and non-western music forms.

The Music Office supports the work of three of Scotland's four national companies, the Scottish Chamber Orchestra, the Royal Scottish National Orchestra and Scottish Opera as well as a number of festivals, music clubs and societies. In addition to revenue and project support for the work of music organisations, the Music Office also offers support to individual artists and composers through bursaries, commissions and training awards.

VISUAL ARTS

The Visual Arts Department supports and promotes the development of contemporary visual art in Scotland. The department funds a number of public galleries, open access printmaking, photography and sculpture workshops, public art agencies and studio provision. Through specific schemes it also offers financial support directly to individual artists and a wide range of projects and events across Scotland. The department is responsible for SAC's own collection of Scottish Contemporary Art which is being gifted to galleries and museums in Scotland as part of a scheme to promote new purchases and commissions.

Organisations and individuals working in the visual arts can receive financial advice and assistance towards: hosting artists' placements; hiring and touring exhibitions; visual arts publications; commissioning art for public display; researching, organising and presenting exhibitions and establishing new posts concerned with the making and promoting of exhibitions.

Individual artists can benefit from awards to develop their work, including international residencies and small assistance grants for exhibitions, materials, transport and travel at home and abroad.

1

National Artists Register

The Visual Arts Department and the Crafts Department have supported the development by Axis of a database which contains information and images on up to 500 artists and craftspeople based in Scotland. Copies of the Axis National Artists Register are held at Hi-Arts in Inverness and at the Centre for Contemporary Arts (CCA) in Glasgow and can be accessed, free of charge on an appointment basis.

The Travelling Gallery

The Visual Arts Department also operates the Travelling Gallery, a gallery in a custom built vehicle which hosts a varied and stimulating programme of exhibitions supported by a range of workshops and educational events designed to introduce visitors to new concepts and techniques. Tours by the Gallery take many months to plan and involve close local liaison with local community groups, teachers and education advisers, local authorities and arts organisations. Itineraries are carefully drawn up to interest different sectors of the community.

THE NATIONAL LOTTERY

The National Lottery provides funding which is designed to achieve the maximum benefit for the general public through support for arts projects which make an important and lasting difference to the quality of life. Lottery funds are available to all art forms, including film, and are primarily directed towards funding building projects, art in public places, film production and equipment purchase. The National Lottery Department of the Scottish Arts Council administers Lottery funding for the arts and film in Scotland and has its own staff and an advisory committee. It is also advised by a number of specialist bodies including the Scottish Film Production Fund and the Scottish Film Council. In its first year of operation, the Scottish Arts Council had £29 million of Lottery funds available for distribution.

2

INFORMATION SERVICES

The Scottish Arts Council acts as an essential source of information and advice to the arts community. It provides an easily accessible Help Desk service, supported by a wide range of information materials, and custom built databases. It also publishes information factsheets, annual reports, research and a two monthly Information Bulletin.

The Help Desk is the starting point for quick reference enquiries on a wide range of arts related topics including: SAC's own activities, funding schemes and publications; contacts in arts and related organisations; sources of funding; training opportunities and arts venues.

The Help Desk can provide information from a number of computerised databases which contain details of key areas of assistance and support for the arts in Scotland. Databases include:

DataTrust: information on trusts and foundations offering funding and other forms of support to the arts;

DataConsult: consultancies which provide general advice or specialist support for artists and arts bodies;

DataEthnic: information on minority ethnic artists and arts organisations based in Scotland;

DataVenue: general, technical and marketing information on Scottish performing arts venues;

DataTour: literary venues, organisations and contacts to assist writers' tours in Scotland.

Development Work

SAC also undertakes a wide range of development work. Recent examples include the establishment of a new agency to fund and provide services to music clubs and amateur promoters; a development programme with local authorities; a major programme to improve arts marketing; work with the Scottish Tourist Board on arts and tourism; a new visual database of the work of Scottish artists and craftspeople.

For enquiries about the arts in Scotland contact:
The Scottish Arts Council,
12 Manor Place, Edinburgh
EH3 7DD
Tel: +44 131 226 6051
Fax:+44 131 225 9833

The Help Desk
Tel: +44 131 243 2444
e-mail:
helpdesk.SAC@artsfb.org.uk

1 'Tanked up Girls', Iced Jems and Jasmin Birtles, Edinburgh Festival Fringe   2 'Still/Here', Bill T Jones/Arnie Zane Dance Company, Edinburgh International Festival

The Scottish Film Council

The Scottish Film Council is the Government funded agency with the remit to promote all aspects of the moving image in Scotland. In 1996/7 it received £1.135 million in grant aid from the Scottish Office.

In April 1996, the Secretary of State for Scotland announced the Government's intention to create a unified Scottish Screen organisation encompassing the work undertaken by the various film organisations in Scotland. Charged with promoting both film as an industry and moving image culture, Scottish Screen will be fully operational by the end of 1997.

The aims of the Film Council are to encourage understanding, appreciation and enjoyment of the film medium, to help production, to preserve the nation's film and television heritage, to promote high quality training and to widen access to all aspects of the moving image. It seeks to achieve this by encouraging production, training and film exhibition and by supporting media education and an information service.

The Scottish Film Council is governed by a Board of eleven directors, the majority of whom are appointed by the Secretary of State for Scotland, and who have responsibility for ensuring that the work of the Council is carried out according to the policies and priorities determined by the Board and staff at the beginning of each year. Directors of the Film Council receive no remuneration for their services, and are responsible for a staff of over 20.

Exhibition

The Scottish Film Council believes that the greatest number of people should be able to see the widest range of films under the best possible conditions. A substantial proportion of SFC's resources are therefore devoted to supporting regional cinemas, such as Glasgow Film Theatre, Edinburgh Filmhouse and the Steps Film Theatre in Dundee, to film societies and to film festivals. Exhibition venues such as these extend the range of films normally available in commercial cinemas and allow film programmes to be more structured and put into context.

Production

The Film Council believes that high levels of film and television production are essential to a healthy moving image culture, allowing the nation of Scotland to express itself to others. The Film Council therefore works to support specialist agencies such as the Scottish Film Production Fund, Scottish Screen Locations and the Glasgow and Edinburgh Producers' Funds in stimulating a Scottish based industry.

The Council actively encourages stability and expansion of production in television and film and works with local authorities to create development funding for independent producers. The Scottish Film Council supports a wide range of film and video workshop organisations throughout Scotland.

Training

The Scottish Film Council plays an important role in developing high quality technical and production training, essential for the industry's creativity and expansion.

The Council has devised a number of initiatives designed to encourage and develop the skills of Scottish writers, directors and producers. The Film Council works closely with schools, colleges, universities and with SCOTVEC, the Scottish Vocational Qualifications awarding body, in the provision of vocational courses. The Film Council was a joint founder of the Scottish industry training body, now called Scottish Broadcast and Film Training Ltd., and financially supports the work of that organisation. The Scottish Film Council is also a partner in the Arts Management Training Initiative Scotland (AMTIS) which develops the skills of Regional Film Theatre staff.

Education and Publishing

The Film Council is a UK leader in the development of Media Education, especially in schools and colleges. A wide range of teaching packs has been written and published and specialist teacher training courses established. The Council was instrumental in creating the Association for Media Education in Scotland and has provided residential training courses for teachers. In addition to media education documents, SFC has an active publications programme which includes the Scottish film book, 'From Limelight to Satellite' and the Bill Douglas monograph 'A Lanternist's Tale'.

Archive

The Scottish Film Council is the home of the Scottish Film Archive. Some four million feet of non-fiction film contained in twenty thousand cans are stored in the vaults, with an associated programme of preservation, restoration and cataloguing. This material represents the moving image history of Scotland and is complemented by an ever growing collection of television programmes, in particular those broadcast in Gaelic. Footage from the Archive is available to programme makers, educational users and students of Scottish culture. The Archive also administers a collection of cinema memorabilia and historical records on Scottish film production.

Information

The Scottish Film Council has also established an information resource service, available to the public and to industry. This resource includes a wide range of periodicals and books, VHS reference copies of Scottish films and television programmes and the Skillset UK training database. The Film Council is host to the Media Antenna for Scotland, where all information relating to the European Union's audio-visual industries development programme can be consulted. In addition to its annual review, the Council publishes newsletters, factsheets and research reports such as the Scottish Screen Data Digest and the Animator's Directory.

For enquiries about film and the screen industries in Scotland contact:
The Scottish Film Council,
74 Victoria Crescent Road,
Glasgow G12 9JN
Tel: +44 141 334 4445
Fax:+44 141 334 8132
e-mail:
SFC@cityscape.co.uk

The other organisations which together with SFC form Scottish Screen are listed on pages 47 and 48.

1 James Cosmo at the launch of 'Scotscreen 100'   2 'Rob Roy'   3 Cinemobile   4 On the set of 'Silent Scream'   Classics from Scottish film - 5 'Whisky Galore', directed by Alexander Mackendrick   6 'Local Hero', directed by Bill Forsyth

Museums and National Institutions

The National Institutions of Scotland are the National Galleries, the National Library and the National Museums of Scotland. They are the responsibility of the Arts and Cultural Heritage Division of the Scottish Office Education and Industry Department. The key objective for all the National Institutions, specified by the Scottish Office, is to ensure that they provide a high quality, cost effective service by improving facilities and increasing public enjoyment of the collections. Together with the Scottish Museums Council, the National Institutions work to create a quality of service and standard of excellence in museums and galleries throughout Scotland.

THE SCOTTISH MUSEUMS COUNCIL

The Scottish Museums Council is the main channel of central Government support for Scotland's 400 museums and art galleries. It is principally funded by the Secretary of State for Scotland, receiving £782,000 in 1996/7, but also receives income from membership subscriptions, fees from training, conservation and consultancy services and donations from charitable organisations.

The remit of the Scottish Museums Council is to improve the quality of museum and gallery provision in Scotland. The Council aims to meet this objective through providing financial assistance to foster excellent standards of performance, forward planning and collections care, the development of good quality museums training and the provision of specialist museums services.

The Scottish Museums Council also provides advice to the Scottish Office on Scottish Museums matters and administers the Museums and Galleries registration scheme in Scotland. The Council has over 200 member organisations including local authorities, armed services museum trusts, Universities, independent museums with charitable status and historic houses. It has a staff of 25.

....

For enquiries about museums in Scotland contact:
The Scottish Museums Council,
County House,
20-22 Torphichen Street,
Edinburgh EH3 8JB
Tel: +44 131 229 7465
Fax: +44 131 229 2728

....

1

THE NATIONAL MUSEUMS OF SCOTLAND

The National Museums of Scotland aim to provide Scotland with a national museum service of international standing which preserves and enhances the collections in its care and promotes research on them so that they can be used to communicate and increase knowledge, understanding and enjoyment of human and natural history.

The Royal Museum of Scotland in Edinburgh houses the international collections in a magnificent Victorian building whose main hall is one of the most impressive public spaces in Scotland. A vast and varied range of objects are on display, from the endangered Giant Panda to working scale models of British steam engines. It mounts exhibitions on jewellery, scientific instruments, costume, European Art, evolution, fossils, Western decorative arts, Japanese and Chinese material, Middle Eastern cultures, mammals, fish, birds and insects.

The Museum of Scotland, next door to the Royal Museum, due to be opened in 1998, will house the collections of Scottish material which tell the story of Scotland's landscape, life and history using the rich and outstanding national collections. The building, designed following a major international competition, will have five floors in which visitors will be able to learn how Scotland was formed, where her first peoples settled, who invaded the land, the early Scottish Kings, the Act of Union in 1707 and the development of the modern Scotland from the early 18th Century.

The Museum of Antiquities in Edinburgh currently displays some of the Scottish collections which will move to the Museum of Scotland. Visitors can see some of the best preserved military and domestic objects from the Roman occupation of Scotland, magnificent Pictish treasures, jewellery and other fascinating objects such as The Maidenùan early beheading machine. The Museum of Antiquities also houses the National Museums of Scotland library.

Shambellie House Museum of Costume at New Abbey, near Dumfries, offers visitors the chance to see period clothes in appropriate settings, with accessories, furniture and decorative art. Shambellie House was designed by the celebrated Scottish architect, David Bryce, and built for the Stewart family in 1856. A dining room scene shows a bride and groom welcoming guests to a summer wedding celebration of 1912, while in the drawing room a ladies' afternoon tea party from the 1890's is taking place. Shambellie House, set in magnificent grounds gives visitors a taste of Society life from the 1890's to the 1920's, and the history of the Stewart family is told in a special display.

The National Museums of Scotland also comprise The Scottish United Services Museum in Edinburgh Castle; the Scottish Agricultural Museum at Ingliston; the Museum of Flight at Ingliston and Biggar Gasworks Museum.

For further information about the National Museums of Scotland contact:
The Royal Museum of Scotland, Chambers Street, Edinburgh EH1 1JF
Tel: +44 131 225 7534
Fax:+44 131 220 4819

THE NATIONAL LIBRARY OF SCOTLAND

The National Library is the largest library in Scotland, with over six million books, and is among the six largest libraries in Britain. It has extensive and varied collections of printed materials and large collections of manuscripts. Its special characteristics derive from its status as a national and legal deposit library. Since 1710 the Library has had the right, under successive Copyright Acts, to acquire all books published in the United Kingdom, and it now seeks to obtain, through legal deposit, books and other publications that are within the scope of the Library's collection development policy. The Library also acquires, mainly by purchase , but also by gift and deposit, older books, maps and music, modern foreign publications and manuscripts. Its primary function is that of general research library. The National Library also stages special exhibitions of books and manuscripts, and exhibitions in photographic form have toured successfully in Scotland and abroad.

For further information about the National Library of Scotland contact:
The National Library of Scotland, George IV Bridge, Edinburgh EH1 1EW
Tel: +44 131 226 4531
Fax:+44 131 220 6662

THE NATIONAL GALLERIES OF SCOTLAND

The National Galleries of Scotland's statutory function relates to the management, development and display of its collections for study and the wider enjoyment of the public. The National Galleries of Scotland consists of three galleries each focusing on discrete subjects and operating in a largely autonomous manner, although subject to the overall control of the Director and ultimately to the Trustees of the National Galleries.

The National Gallery of Scotland (1859) on The Mound in Edinburgh contains one of the finest small collections of painting, prints and drawings in Europe, and its master pieces - from pre-Renaissance to Post-Impressionism - include works by Raphael, Velasquez, Rembrandt, Turner, Degas and Van Gogh. It is also the home of the world's finest collection of Scottish painting from Ramsay to Raeburn and McTaggart. The National Gallery covers European painting, drawing and sculpture from the medieval period until approximately 1900.

Although the Royal Scottish Academy building is partly occupied by the Academy, an independent body, the National Galleries of Scotland is responsible for the management of the building which contains its major facility for temporary exhibitions.

The Scottish National Portrait Gallery is housed in the Findlay Building in Queen Street, Edinburgh, and also hosts part of the collection of the National Museums. The Portrait Gallery contains portraits of famous Scots from the sixteenth century to the present day, ranging from Mary Queen of Scots and Bonnie Prince Charlie to Hugh MacDiarmid and Sir Alexander Gibson. The National Portrait Gallery also contains collections of topographical paintings and paintings of contemporary historical events, and houses the Scottish Photography Archive.

The Scottish National Gallery of Modern Art, situated in Belford Road, Edinburgh covers international painting, drawing and sculpture from approximately 1900 to the present day, and houses examples of the best of Scottish Modern Art from Bellany, Peploe, Paolozzi and Joan Eardley alongside works by Picasso, Matisse, Hockney and Henry Moore.

The National Galleries also have permanent displays from their collections in two country houses, Paxton House, in the Borders and Duff House in Grampian.

For further information about the National Galleries of Scotland contact:
The National Gallery of Scotland, The Mound, Edinburgh EH2 2EL
Tel: +44 131 556 8921
Fax:+44 131 556 9972

Development and Funding

In addition to the main grant awarding bodies, funded by Government, there are a number of agencies and organisations which offer advice and assistance to arts organisations.

ASSOCIATION FOR BUSINESS SPONSORSHIP OF THE ARTS

The Association for Business Sponsorship of the Arts (ABSA) Scotland exists to promote and encourage partnerships between the private sector and the arts, to their mutual benefit and to that of the community at large. ABSA works with organisations to provide a range of different services.

Services to Arts Organisations

Includes introduction to sponsorship seminars, individual surgeries and advice on sponsorship proposals and databases of sponsors and sponsorship opportunities. ABSA has an Arts Services Manager jointly funded with the Scottish Arts Council.

Business in the Arts

Offers a placement scheme through which business managers with relevant skills are recruited and trained and subsequently placed on a part time, voluntary basis with arts organisations to help with particular management projects. A management training initiative offers free or low cost business training courses for arts managers, and a Board Bank is operated which is a confidential register of people with business skills offering to share their experience with arts organisations by serving on their boards.

Pairing Scheme

A Government scheme administered by ABSA which offers matching funds for new or increased sponsorship money.

ABSA Awards

ABSA Scottish Awards for Business Sponsorship of the Arts. An annual awards ceremony and gala event to celebrate the best in arts sponsorship in Scotland. Specially commissioned awards are given in seven categories.

For further information contact:
The Director, ABSA Scotland, 100 Wellington Street, Glasgow G2 6PB.
Tel: +44 141 204 3864
Fax: +44 141 204 3897

1

INTERNATIONAL CULTURAL DESK

The International Cultural Desk is an independent organisation, jointly established in 1994 by The British Council, the Scottish Arts Council and the Scottish Museums Council with additional funding from Scottish Enterprise National and the Highlands and Islands Enterprise. Its aim is to assist the Scottish arts and cultural community to operate more effectively in an international context by providing timely and targeted information and advice. The Desk deals with all art forms and art practices, including museums and galleries, but excluding film, where the Scottish Film Council provides its own information service. Concentrating initially on countries in Europe and North America, it is planned that the Desk will eventually expand to cover countries in Australasia, Central and South America and Asia and Africa. Staff provide information and advice about international funding sources, networks, residencies, partners for collaboration, conferences, festivals and other opportunities in the international arena. The Desk publishes a bi-monthly information update 'Communication', which lists forthcoming opportunities for the Scottish arts and cultural sector, and produces topical and sectoral factsheets. It also runs seminars and offers surgeries for arts organisations to receive in-depth advice from experts on aspects of international cultural matters.

For further information contact:
The Development Manager, International Cultural Desk, 6 Belmont Crescent, Glasgow G12 8ES
Tel: +44 141 339 0090
Fax:+44 141 337 2271
e-mail:
icd@dial.pipex.com

2

3

SCOTTISH ARTS LOBBY

The Scottish Arts Lobby, SALVO, (Scottish Arts Lobby Voice) is a federation of some 300 arts organisations and local authorities throughout Scotland. Its members are large and small, professional and amateur and are from urban and rural communities. SALVO is an independent organisation, funded solely by membership subscription. It is a non-party political organisation with observers from all the parliamentary parties.

SALVO exists to lobby and exerts firm, constructive and informed pressure on the political system on behalf of the cultural sector. It provides its members with information, advice and support, holding seminars and conferences, developing policies and advising public agencies and Government on cultural issues and legislative proposals.

For further information contact:
The Director, SALVO, c/o The Royal Lyceum Theatre, Grindlay Street, Edinburgh EH3 9AX
Tel: +44 131 228 3885
Fax:+44 131 228 3955

SCOTTISH TOURIST BOARD

Tourism is one of Scotland's largest industries, employing 180,000 people (8% of the workforce) and injecting £2 billion annually into the economy.

The Scottish Tourist Board was established under the Development of Tourism Act 1969, to attract visitors to Scotland and encourage them to travel widely within Scotland. The Scottish Tourist Board aims to promote the highest standards of service, hospitality and training. As the leading marketing agency in tourism, the Board works closely with the private sector and with the various statutory agencies whose activities affect tourism. Regular liaison is maintained with the British Tourist Authority on the promotion of Scotland in overseas markets. The Board is financed by Government, through the Scottish Office and derives revenue from the sale of publications and through the provision of specialist services.

The quality and range of the arts in Scotland is a unique tourism asset. The Scottish Tourist Board participates in a Tourism and the Arts Taskforce alongside the Scottish Arts Council and other public agencies, development bodies and local authorities to develop links between the arts and tourism. A National Co-ordinator, based at the Scottish Tourist Board, encourages arts organisations to promote themselves to tourists and tourism agencies to promote the arts. A number of issues have been addressed by the Taskforce including the encouragement of the accessibility of high quality arts and tourism information for both visitors and the travel trade, the creation of direct links with the overseas travel trade, and the encouragement of the development of new and existing tourism and arts activities and venues.

For further information about the arts and tourism contact:
The National Co-ordinator, Arts and Tourism Scotland, The Scottish Tourist Board, 23 Ravelston Terrace, Edinburgh EH4 3EU
Tel: +44 131 332 2433
Fax:+44 131 343 2023

4

5

SCOTLAND THE BRAND

Scotland the Brand is a pilot project to increase the effectiveness of marketing Scotland internationally by integrating trade, tourism and the arts in co-operative promotions overseas. The project is jointly funded by The British Council, Scottish Trade International and the Scottish Tourist Board. Special promotions have taken place in key overseas trade areas involving an arts element, which is conceived as integral to the success of the promotions, and which comprise programmed performances and activities relevant to the specific market and scope of each campaign.

For further information about Scotland the Brand contact:
The Director, Scotland the Brand, 64 Waterloo Street, Glasgow G2 7DE
Tel: +44 141 225 2005
Fax:+44 141 225 2003

NATIONAL ENTERPRISE AGENCIES

Scottish Enterprise and Highlands and Islands Enterprise are the two main economic development agencies for Scotland and each has a network of local enterprise companies (LEC's) throughout Scotland responsible for development and training. Scottish Enterprise, under various schemes, has occasionally assisted specific developments in the cultural sector, where these represent an additional benefit to the economy through, for example, tourism. Highlands and Islands Enterprise (HIE) has a responsibility for economic development which includes a specific social remit enabling support to be given to cultural activities in addition to its specific remit for cultural tourism, as identified through Objective 1 funding from the European Union. In order to develop the cultural infrastructure in the Highlands and Islands, Highlands and Islands Enterprise has produced an arts strategy.

An arts development officer is jointly funded by the Scottish Arts Council and Highlands and Islands Enterprise to take forward the arts strategy through liaison and co-operation between the HIE/Local Enterprise Company Network and all other relevant groups, agencies and individuals in the area. The Arts Development Officer is housed in Hi-Arts, an independent arts promotion company based in Inverness.

Hi-Arts maintains a database on Highland arts organisations, produces the quarterly arts listing newspaper De Tha Dol, helps to co-ordinate performing arts in the Highlands and Islands and is able to undertake a broad range of arts development activities.

LOCAL ENTERPRISE COMPANIES

Local enterprise companies serve a local area, as part of a network of economic development agencies and are responsible to either Scottish Enterprise National or Highlands and Islands Enterprise. A number of local enterprise companies have assisted cultural developments in the arts, for example, the Edinburgh Festival Theatre was financially assisted by Lothian and Edinburgh Enterprise.

For further information about the National Enterprise Agencies contact:
Scottish Enterprise, 120 Bothwell Street, Glasgow G2 7JP
Tel: +44 141 248 2700
Fax:+44 141 221 3217
e-mail
scotentcsd@scotent.co.uk

Highlands and Islands Enterprise, Bridge House, 20 Bridge Street, Inverness IV1 1QR
Tel: +44 1463 234171
Fax:+44 1463 244469

Education

Education and the arts are inextricably linked. The arts are essential to the development of individual expression and creativity, and education is an integral part of the work of most arts organisations. The expressive arts are built into the school curriculum from an early age and there are a number of educational establishments which offer third level and in-service courses in specific art forms and disciplines for those who have decided to pursue a career in the arts.

ARTS MANAGEMENT TRAINING INITIATIVE SCOTLAND
Funded by the main cultural agencies, AMTIS was established to provide an annual programme of short courses for cultural workers to enable them to enhance their managerial competence; to create opportunities for continuing professional development and to support the growth and development of Scotland's arts and cultural services sector. In addition to the short course programme, AMTIS has been instrumental in establishing three parallel post degree programmes which are run by Heriot Watt University in Edinburgh:

MSc Cultural Services
Management
(2 years part time);
MSc Cultural Policy
(1 year full time);
MBA Cultural Sector
Management Option
(part and full time).

These degrees are awarded by Heriot-Watt University, and a distance learning option for the MSc in Cultural Services Management is also available for cultural workers in the Highlands and Islands.
From April 1996 there will be new arrangements in place for short course training and enquiries should be directed to the Scottish Arts Council.

ROYAL SCOTTISH ACADEMY OF MUSIC AND DRAMA (Glasgow)
The mission of the Royal Scottish Academy of Music and Drama (RSAMD), based in Glasgow, is to produce musicians, opera singers, actors and other professionals in music and drama well equipped to pursue a diverse choice of careers at national and international level.
The Academy was granted degree awarding powers in 1994 which has enabled it to strengthen its main purpose of providing vocational training of the highest quality at degree level for the music and drama professions. The Academy also mounts many student and professional performances and productions throughout the year in each of its four principal auditoria.

For further information contact:
RSAMD, 100 Renfrew Street,
Glasgow G2 3DB
Tel: +44 141 332 4101
Fax:+44 141 332 8901

QUEEN MARGARET COLLEGE (Edinburgh)
The Drama Department offers four full time courses, all of which are geared to the expanding and challenging employment opportunities in the arts and entertainment industries. Three courses, a BA(Hons) in Acting, a BA (Hons) in Stage Management and Theatre run in association with the Royal Lyceum Theatre and a BA Hons in Combined Studies (Theatre Studies) are offered as 3/4 year full time courses. The fourth, a PgDip in Community Theatre run in association with Theatre Workshop, is offered as a one year full time course or a two year part time option.
The Department of Drama also has a growing community of doctoral researchers. During the academic year, the Department produces over 12 shows in the fully equipped College theatre, as well as presenting productions on tour and in Lothian schools. The Drama Department is a member of the Conference of Drama Schools and the Standing Committee of University Drama Departments.

For further information contact:
Admissions Office, Queen
Margaret College, Clerwood
Terrace, Edinburgh EH12 8TS
Tel: +44 131 317 3247
Fax:+44 131 317 3256

DUNCAN OF JORDANSTONE COLLEGE OF ART (Dundee)
A Faculty of the University of Dundee, Duncan of Jordanstone College of Art offers a broad range of honours degree programmes within the Fine Arts and Design areas. These include Painting, Sculpture, Printmaking, Time Based Art, Graphic Design, Illustration and Printmaking, Printed Textiles, Constructed Textiles, Interior and Environmental Design, Ceramics, Jewellery and Metalwork and Animation and Electronic Media. At postgraduate level there is a Master of Fine Art (MFA) programme and a Master of Design (MDes). The programmes in Time Based Art and Animation and Electronic Media are offered by the Schools of Fine Art and Design respectively in co-operation with the School of Television and Imaging which also offers a Postgraduate Diploma in Electronic Imaging.
The College has student exchange agreements for Art and Design with colleges and

32

universities in Canada, the USA, Italy, France, Holland and Sweden and numerous exchanges, mainly for third year students, take place each year.

For further information contact: Duncan of Jordanstone College, The University of Dundee, 13 Perth Road, Dundee DD1 4HT
Tel: +44 1382 345713
Fax:+44 1382 227304

EDINBURGH COLLEGE OF ART (Edinburgh)

Edinburgh College of Art offers a wide range of degree courses in the fields of Art and Design and Environmental Studies. There are four Schools in the Faculty of Art and Design: the Schools of Design and Applied Arts (with specialist subjects in Ceramics, Fashion and Theatre Costume, Furniture, Glass and Architectural Glass, Interior Design, Jewellery and Silversmithing, Printed Textiles); Drawing and Painting (with specialist subjects in Painting, Printmaking and Tapestry); Sculpture; and Visual Communication (with specialist subjects in Animation, Film/TV, Graphic Design, Illustration and Photography). There are three Schools in the Faculty of Environmental Studies: Architecture; Landscape Architecture and Planning and Housing.

Throughout the year the College runs a varied exhibition programme within the College's galleries and exhibition spaces which include the Sculpture Court and the Andrew Grant Gallery as well as numerous spaces provided by the Schools and Departments. All exhibitions are open to the public and

feature the work of students and staff as well as touring or specially curated exhibitions of local, UK or international origin. The exhibitions programme culminates in June with the Annual Degree Show which features the work of all graduating students. The College also hosts major exhibitions during the Edinburgh International Festival.

Over the years, the College has developed strong educational links in Europe and North America, expanding more recently in some Schools to include South America, Australia, China and Pakistan, providing opportunities for study visits and student exchanges.

For further information contact: The Development Officer, Edinburgh College of Art, Lauriston Place, Edinburgh EH3 9DF
Tel: +44 131 221 6000
Fax:+44 131 221 6001
e-mail:
p.swann@eca.ac.uk

GLASGOW SCHOOL OF ART (Glasgow)

The Glasgow School of Art is one of the very few remaining independent art schools in the United Kingdom. Founded in 1845 as a Government School of Design, the study and practice of the fine arts and architecture became part of the curriculum towards the end of the 19th Century. The School has occupied its present building since 1899 and at the heart of the campus is Charles Rennie Mackintosh's masterwork now known as the Mackintosh Building. Mackintosh, one of

the School's former pupils, was commissioned in 1896 to design this building to provide a home for the School. It has subsequently become a place of pilgrimage for visitors from around the world but remains fundamentally a working art school.

The School of Art comprises four schools: Architecture; Design; Fine Art; Core Studies and the Department of Historical and Critical Studies. The School of Design and Craft offers seven specialisms: Ceramics; Embroidered and Woven Textiles; Graphic Design and Photography; Interior Design; Product Design; Printed and Knitted Textiles and Silversmithing and Jewellery. The School of Fine Art offers specialisms in Environmental Art; Painting; Photography; Printmaking and Sculpture. Courses offered range from undergraduate through to higher degrees by research. The School owns and maintains a substantial archive of international significance, and the Mackintosh Building and Collection represent a large research and teaching asset. There are two large galleries as well as a number of exhibition areas which are used both for students and to the benefit of the City and the wider community.

The School operates a variety of student exchange programmes with institutions world-wide, particularly in North America and Europe. Both the Mackintosh School of Architecture and the School of Design and Craft have established Erasmus programmes and opportunities therefore exist

for students to participate in structured exchanges.

For further information contact: Glasgow School of Art, 167 Renfrew Street, Glasgow G3 6RQ
Tel: +44 141 353 4500
Fax:+44 141 353 4746

GRAYS COLLEGE OF ART (Aberdeen)

Part of the Robert Gordon University and established in 1885, Gray's School of Art has achieved a high national and international reputation. Located in purpose-built facilities in parkland on the banks of the River Dee, students work and study in spacious studios, supported by the latest technology. Tutors in Fine Art, Design and Craft and Design for Industry are active and successful practitioners, and students are increasingly successful in major competitions. The Research Unit has growing numbers researching at MA, MPhil and PhD levels across the spectrum of art and design subject areas.

Though noted for its strong links with local and regional communities, Gray's regularly hosts international seminars and visits from eminent designers and artists.

For further information contact: The Head of School, The Robert Gordon University, Gray's School of Art, Garthdee Road, Aberdeen AB10 9QD
Tel: +44 1224 263601
Fax:+44 1224 263636

Arts organisations in Scotland

Scotland's arts organisations are funded by the Scottish Arts Council; local authorities; sponsorship from business, charitable trusts, trade unions and private individuals; and earned income. In order to obtain funding, an arts organisation will generally be set up as a limited company with charitable status, and have a board of Directors drawn from the public who have a range of skills useful to that organisation. The Directors are charged with the responsibility of ensuring that the company uses the money which it is granted efficiently and effectively and for the purpose for which it was offered. It is the organisation's Directors who are accountable to the funding bodies for the money which has been granted.

At present, the Scottish Arts Council is funded by the Scottish Office on an annual basis, and this is reflected in the Council's on going revenue grants to arts organisations. Each revenue funded organisation is required to submit each year a four year plan to the Scottish Arts Council. Such plans are then scrutinised by the relevant officers and committees of the Scottish Arts Council against the Council's own determined policies and priorities, and an assessment of the quality of the work, before the final grant determination is made. In this way, the use of public money to fund the arts is made accountable, and ensures that arts funding in Scotland is part of a strategic process to make the arts available and accessible to all. Other organisations are funded on a project by project basis with no expectation of funding continuing in the future.

FESTIVALS

Scotland has many festivals, ranging in length from three weeks to just one day and from international to local themes. It is this variety and diversity of cultural activity which gives Scotland its own unique cultural life. The following are some of the main cultural festivals which take place throughout Scotland:

1

2

ABERDEEN ALTERNATIVE FESTIVAL (Aberdeen)

The Aberdeen Alternative Festival takes place annually in October, and is an international event, blending the rich cultural heritage of the North East of Scotland with an eclectic mix of world cultures. World class artists of the calibre of Art Blakey, Michael Nyman, Stephane Grappelli and Van Morrison have featured as headline acts, while the Festival continues to widen its appeal with contemporary dance, drama, comedy and street theatre together with a broad based traditional arts programme of masterclasses, workshops and ceilidhs. An innovative community arts programme forms a major part of the Festival, offering a wide range of participatory projects, events and workshops across the City, in conjunction with local communities.

ABERDEEN INTERNATIONAL YOUTH FESTIVAL (Aberdeen)

The Aberdeen International Youth Festival is held annually during the first two weeks of August. Run by the Aberdeen International Youth Festival Trust and established in 1973, the Festival is open to leading youth symphony and chamber orchestras, choirs, jazz groups, dance (ballet, traditional and contemporary) and drama groups. The maximum age for participants is 25 years and all groups must be of amateur status.

The Festival is truly international and groups come from all over the world to participate, living in Aberdeen University during the fortnight. The groups give major performances in the City of Aberdeen and also tour to venues throughout the North East of Scotland. Great emphasis is placed on the young people getting to know each other and there is a nightly Festival Club where they perform informally to each other.

The Festival also runs two residential summer schools in

1 Scottish Children's Festival 2 'Appetite', Club Swing, Citizens' Theatre, Mayfest

August for young dancers and musicians, holds an annual visual arts project involving sculptors and printmakers, runs its own youth choir and co-ordinates a performing arts programme every other year involving local young disabled people.

BORDERS FESTIVAL (Borders)

A biennial festival held in October which celebrates the cultural heritage of the Borders, the Borders Festival uses local artists, writers and performers in a festival which encompasses music, dance, drama and the visual arts in venues throughout the Borders.

CELTIC CONNECTIONS (Glasgow)

Celtic Connections is a two week festival of Celtic music from all corners of the globe, organised and promoted by the Glasgow Royal Concert Hall in January of each year. Offering a varied programme of music performances, workshops, masterclasses and lectures, Celtic Connections showcases the best of Scottish traditional and contemporary music alongside artists from Ireland, America, Wales, Brittany and further afield. Since its establishment in 1993, the Festival has expanded from its base in the Concert Hall to encompass venues elsewhere in the City, including a very popular Festival Club. The Celtic Connections Festival attracts audiences in excess of 90,000 per annum.

DRAMBUIE EDINBURGH FILM FESTIVAL (Edinburgh)

Based in Edinburgh, this is the oldest continuously running film festival in the world, having been in existence for over 50 years. Born as a festival of documentary film making, Edinburgh became known for its championing of genre and exploitation cinema, especially in the 60's with its focus on Minelli, Scorsese and Fuller. Special features on Women's, Third World and Japanese cinema have also enhanced its world wide reputation. The Festival invites creative film makers of all types to submit their new work and compete for its prizes for Best British Feature, Best British Animation, Best Rosebud (world premiere) film etc. The Film Festival takes place during August every year, and offers a spectacular round of premieres, galas, lectures, masterclasses and opportunities to meet the stars behind the movies being shown.

EDINBURGH INTERNATIONAL FESTIVAL (Edinburgh)

The Edinburgh International Festival of the arts is held annually from mid August to early September. The programme of events features the very best in international theatre, music, dance and opera. The Edinburgh International Festival aims to reflect international culture in presentation to Scottish audiences and Scottish culture in presentation to international audiences. It brings together a programme of events in an innovative way that cannot easily be achieved by other organisations and provides one of the few opportunities for thousands of performers from around the world to bring their collective talent to a huge and appreciative audience.

EDINBURGH FESTIVAL FRINGE (Edinburgh)

The Edinburgh Festival Fringe is the world's largest open arts festival where anyone can participate, and which runs for three weeks in mid August through to early September, alongside the Edinburgh International Festival. The Society runs a central box office for all performances; publishes a comprehensive programme of events and offers year round advice and assistance for all prospective performers. The joy of the Fringe is in the multiplicity of artists, art forms, performances and venues which can keep the dedicated festival goer busy from first thing in the morning until last thing at night.

EDINBURGH BOOK FESTIVAL (Edinburgh)

A biennial event, the Book Festival runs for two weeks in mid August, during the Edinburgh International Festival, on uneven years. Situated in the gardens of the Georgian Charlotte Square in the West end of the City, the Edinburgh Book Festival offers a wide programme of readings, lectures and events for both adults and children in addition to having an extensive range of Scottish and other books for sale.

EDINBURGH INTERNATIONAL JAZZ AND BLUES FESTIVAL (Edinburgh)

A one week festival coinciding with the first week of the Edinburgh International Festival, the Edinburgh International Jazz and Blues Festival provides a showcase for the best of British and international jazz and blues artists.

EDINBURGH PUPPET AND ANIMATION FESTIVAL (Edinburgh)

A one week festival in March/April of puppet shows and workshops with Scottish companies held annually in the Netherbow Arts Centre in Edinburgh.

FOTOFEIS (Scotland)

A biennial international festival of photography in Scotland, Fotofeis stages a festival of photo based arts with a reputation for quality and innovation both locally and internationally. Taking place throughout Scotland in odd numbered years, Fotofeis aims to engage with and afford access for a wide audience while gaining a reputation amongst specialists for excellence, originality, friendliness and the imaginative integration of the international with the local.

FOLK FESTIVALS (Scotland)

Scotland is richly endowed with songs in Scots, Gaelic and English and our interest in traditional music and singing is amply demonstrated by the plethora of folk festivals across the country ranging from the Arran Fleadh and the Balnain

House Summer Festival of Music to the Highland Traditional Music Festival and the Glasgow International Folk Festival. There are folk festivals in Scotland in almost every month of the year, some focusing on local musicians and others containing musicians from all over Scotland, England, Ireland and elsewhere in the world.

GLASGOW INTERNATIONAL JAZZ FESTIVAL
(Glasgow)

A ten day annual festival held in late June, the Glasgow International Jazz Festival promotes the best of Scottish and international contemporary jazz throughout the city in large venues, pubs and clubs as well as in community centres.

HIGHLAND FESTIVAL
(Inverness and the Highlands)

The Highland Festival is a new, annual event held in late May and early June. The festival comprises a pan-highland series of events over a two week period, focusing on seven different areas in the Highlands. The artists and craftspeople of the Highlands form the nucleus of the Festival, and it is their culture and creativity which the Festival celebrates and promotes. Encompassing all the arts, the Highland Festival is a large scale event, both in geographical and artistic terms, and in addition to performances and exhibitions, has a substantial educational programme.

MAYFEST
(Glasgow)

Centred around three weeks in May, Mayfest is a festival of the performing arts which was founded in 1982 out of a unique collaboration between the entertainment unions, the Scottish Trades Union Congress and the Glasgow Trades Council in association with the City of Glasgow District Council. Mayfest has strong links with local communities and the trade union and labour movement in the west of Scotland, and aims to produce a festival which is a true reflection of the best of local and international popular theatre and music. Working with artists, local groups and venues and business, Mayfest is a people's festival, for the people of Glasgow and beyond.

ROYAL NATIONAL MOD
(Scotland)

The Royal National Mod is an annual festival celebrating through competition the best of Scotland's literary, music and vocal talents as expressed through Scotland's national Gaelic language. Taking place in a different town or city throughout Scotland each October, the Mod is attended by over 15,000 adults and children.

NEW MOVES
(Glasgow)

New Moves is a dance festival in Glasgow that offers a showcase of creativity, celebrating Europe and Canada's exciting and often uncompromising young talent. New Moves actively seeks new ways to educate, stimulate and inspire. It strives to attract new audiences, especially those who feel that dance is "not for them". Utilising the Tramway and other venues in Glasgow, New Moves defines new directions in dance, revealing an eclectic range of influences and styles and commissioning new work for some of Scotland's leading dancers and choreographers.

SAINT MAGNUS FESTIVAL
(Orkney)

The St. Magnus Festival was founded in 1977 by Sir Peter Maxwell Davies who is now the Festival's President. Promoting the work of contemporary composers, writers and artists, placing a natural emphasis on work being produced in Scotland, the Festival aims to bring to Orkney professional performances of the highest calibre, whilst at the same time seeking to encourage the maximum degree of local participation by adults and young people. Whilst music events are at the heart of the programme, the Festival also encompasses dance, drama, the visual arts and the spoken word. The Festival is a compact six day annual event taking place in midsummer (June) when the natural light in Orkney is a very special addition to the Festival.

SCOTTISH INTERNATIONAL CHILDREN'S FESTIVAL
(Edinburgh)

A combined arts festival for children aged from 3 to 14, the Scottish International Children's Festival takes place in a tented village in Inverleith Park in Edinburgh. The festival offers a variety of Scottish and international music, dance and drama performances especially produced for children.

For contact details of the arts festivals listed above contact: The Help Desk, The Scottish Arts Council, 12 Manor Place, Edinburgh EH3 7DD
Tel: +44 131 243 2444
Fax: +44 131 477 7241
e-mail:
helpdesk.SAC@artsfb.org.uk

For information about film festivals in Scotland contact: The Scottish Film Council, 74, Victoria Crescent Road, Glasgow G12 9JN
Tel: +44 141 334 4445
Fax: +44 141 334 8132
e-mail:
SFC@cityscape.co.uk

MUSIC

There are hundreds of singers, musicians and musical groups in Scotland, ranging from the very large opera company to the small, but equally professional traditional musician, from small classical ensembles to new music groups, jazz bands and rock groups. The following is a selection of some of the organisations operating in Scotland.

ASSEMBLY DIRECT
(Edinburgh and Scotland)
Assembly Direct promotes jazz and blues throughout Scotland, England and Europe through the organisation of jazz concerts ranging from club gigs to concert hall performances and festivals. Festivals organised by Assembly Direct include the Dundee Jazz Festival in June and the Round Midnight Jazz Festival in Edinburgh held in the Queen's Hall in Edinburgh during the last week of the Edinburgh Festival Fringe.

BBC SCOTTISH SYMPHONY ORCHESTRA
(Glasgow and Scotland)
The BBC Scottish Symphony Orchestra was founded in 1935 as Scotland's first full-time professional orchestra. Originally studio based the orchestra now has an ever increasing public concert schedule throughout the United Kingdom. It appears annually at the BBC Proms in London and at the Edinburgh International Festival, and also makes frequent tours abroad. Contemporary music has always occupied an important place in the orchestra's repertoire, both through an extensive commissioning programme and especially in its support for Scottish composers. Its expertise in performing 20th Century music has led organisations to entrust it with important and demanding projects like the performance of Schoenberg's Moses und Aaron at the 1992 Edinburgh Festival and the 1995 UK premiere of Emmanuel Nunes' complex Quodlibet. Almost all of the orchestra's public concerts and studio performances are broadcast on the BBC's radio or television services, principally Radio Three.

In recent years the BBC Scottish Symphony Orchestra has recorded extensively, winning two Gramophone Awards.

EDINBURGH CONTEMPORARY ARTS TRUST
(Edinburgh and Scotland)
The Edinburgh Contemporary Arts Trust (ECAT) is a charitable organisation promoting the performance, composition and enjoyment of new music in Scotland. Headed by three composers - Geoffrey King, James MacMillan and Peter Nelson- ECAT aims to present the work of Scottish musicians in an international context and initiates a wide variety of events, involving composers, performers and promoters in collaborative ventures in Scotland and abroad. ECAT has been responsible for the commissioning of over 50 new works, mainly from Scottish based composers, and presents a winter season of contemporary music concerts.

ENTERPRISE MUSIC SCOTLAND
(Aberdeen and Scotland)
Enterprise Music Scotland supports the co-ordination, maintenance and development of live music performances through the network of voluntary music promoting organisations in Scotland by means of the provision of financial assistance for live music performances, usually chamber music. It assists in the co-ordination of touring arrangements for music groups and publishes annually the Scottish Tours Book. Enterprise Music Scotland supports new organisations who wish to promote live music performances within their own communities.

NATIONAL YOUTH ORCHESTRA OF SCOTLAND
(Glasgow and Scotland)
The National Youth Orchestra of Scotland offers orchestral and jazz training from distinguished professional musicians, and prepares programmes for performance throughout Scotland and abroad. NYOS arranges community activities to stimulate the teaching and appreciation of music in conjunction with local authorities. In addition to the main orchestral courses and chamber orchestra, the Easter training and summer jazz courses give students the chance to broaden their skills. The National Youth Orchestra of Scotland gives concert tours in December and January and in July and August.

Camerata Scotland, the NYOS pre-professional chamber orchestra gives concert tours world wide. Young people from regional and schools orchestras all over Scotland are auditioned for the NYOS.

PARAGON ENSEMBLE
(Glasgow and Scotland)
Paragon Ensemble aims to maintain a regular performing company of the highest calibre and to present a programme of performances throughout the year, featuring contemporary music and other music of the 20th Century. Paragon strives to reach every area of the public and tries to create an environment where contemporary music is not only accepted, but also sought after, as a stimulating part of everyday life. To assist in this aim, the company presents a series of community projects relating to each concert season presented. Groups targeted for community projects include children, the unemployed, the elderly and those with disabilities. Paragon under takes performances in chamber music, music theatre, opera, film music and music for dance. A crossover with other expressive art forms, such as visual art, also adds to innovative performances. The commissioning of new work is central to Paragon's activities and exposes the talents of new and more established composers in Scotland. International composers also play a large part in Paragon's repertoire, from Eastern Europe, the Far East, USA and Central Europe.

ROYAL SCOTTISH NATIONAL ORCHESTRA
(Glasgow and Scotland)

The Royal Scottish National Orchestra is an 89 member symphony orchestra which is the major provider of symphonic music of the highest international quality throughout Scotland. The orchestra tours in Scotland, the UK and abroad, and presents regular seasons of concerts in Edinburgh, Aberdeen, Dundee and Perth between October and June each year. It supports all of its work with an extensive range of education and outreach work. The RSNO is an active commissioner and performer of new music.

SCOTTISH CHAMBER ORCHESTRA
(Edinburgh and Scotland)

The Scottish Chamber Orchestra is dedicated to the performance, creation and appreciation of music throughout Scotland. An orchestra of 37 players, it gives concerts across Scotland, Britain and abroad in addition to recording, broadcasting and running a busy development programme of concerts and workshops in schools and the wider community. The orchestra undertakes regular winter seasons in Edinburgh, Glasgow, Aberdeen and St. Andrews, and a Highland tour in the summer. An innovative orchestra, the SCO works to encourage the creation and performance of new music. It won the prestigious Prudential Award for Innovation and Access in 1990.

SCOTTISH MUSIC INFORMATION CENTRE
(Glasgow)

The Scottish Music Information Centre (SMIC) documents and promotes music by Scottish and Scottish based composers.

The Centre has a large reference library and sound archive, many of whose items are available for loan upon the presentation of a small fee. The Scottish Music Information Centre publishes the Scottish Music Handbook, and a monthly newsletter about new music in Scotland, and also offers copying and binding facilities. An invaluable resource, SMIC offers a free information service to enquirers.

SCOTTISH OPERA
(Glasgow and Scotland)

Scottish Opera is Scotland's only national opera company and has a full time orchestra and chorus. The company's aim is to stand, at home and abroad, for quality, challenge and popular appeal. Each season, Scottish Opera gives some 80 main scale performances at venues in Glasgow, Aberdeen, Inverness, Edinburgh and Newcastle. The company also offers over 50 medium and small scale performances by Scottish Opera Go Round at smaller venues not able to accommodate large scale opera. The company's educational unit, Scottish Opera for All, also works extensively in the community.

TRADITIONAL MUSIC AND SONG ASSOCIATION OF SCOTLAND
(Edinburgh and Scotland)

The Traditional Music and Song Association (TMSA) promotes the interests of traditional music and song in Scotland through a network of regional branches. The Association promotes the presentation of Scottish traditional music and song and the furtherance of interest in this, hitherto largely oral medium. The TMSA is compiling a national database of artists, and organises national projects. Each year, a calendar of members events is produced detailing folk festivals, workshops and other related activities.

For contact details of the music organisations listed above contact:
The Help Desk, The Scottish Arts Council, 12 Manor Place, Edinburgh EH3 7DD
Tel: +44 131 243 2444
Fax:+44 131 477 7241
e-mail:
helpdesk.SAC@artsfb.org.uk

DRAMA

Scotland boasts an outstanding range of drama companies from building based repertory theatres to touring companies to smaller, project related companies whose activities take place when specific ideas are brought to fruition. The main building based repertory companies are:

BRUNTON THEATRE, MUSSELBURGH
(East Lothian)

Owned and operated by the East Lothian Council, the Brunton Theatre is set in the heart of the Civic Centre of Musselburgh and is undergoing a programme of refurbishment with assistance from the National Lottery. The Brunton Theatre produces a professional programme of contemporary drama, with an emphasis on youth and community work which takes place both in the theatre and in the localities of East Lothian.

BYRE THEATRE, ST ANDREWS
(Fife)

The Byre Theatre serves St Andrews and Fife with a varied programme of drama activity from a professional company which both plays in the main theatre and tours throughout Fife. The Byre Theatre also plays host to visiting small scale theatre companies and works with local writers groups, the St Andrews Youth theatre and young playwrights to develop educational opportunities.

CITIZENS' THEATRE
(Glasgow)

Based in Glasgow, the Citizens' Theatre aims to achieve the highest artistic standards in repertoire, direction, design, acting and the technical aspects of theatre production. Under the artistic direction of Giles Havergal, Philip Prowse and Robert David McDonald, the Citizens' Theatre has built an international reputation for innovative work and for important translations of modern and classical European work in the mainstream tradition. The Citizens theatre building consists of a main proscenium arch auditorium, and two smaller studio theatres. The Citizens Theatre has toured abroad on several occasions to festivals, and has had a number of productions transfer into the commercial arena of the West End of London.

DUNDEE REP THEATRE COMPANY
(Dundee)

Housed in the centre of Dundee, the Dundee Rep Theatre Company presents work from the classical repertoire translated by contemporary Scottish playwrights as well as new Scottish work. Dundee Rep works to increase access of the local community to performing arts through an extensive community drama programme, and also hosts a number of visiting professional drama companies whose work complements that of the producing company. In recent years, the company has mounted a number of professional co-productions with other companies. It is also the home of Scottish Dance Theatre, Scotland's contemporary dance company.

PERTH THEATRE
(Perth)

The oldest repertory theatre in Scotland, Perth Theatre seeks to provide Perth and the surrounding area with live theatre of high quality, making a significant contribution to the life of the community, while developing educational and youth theatre work, and by developing its contribution to Scottish theatre and Scottish culture. The theatre offers a subscription series of five plays each autumn and spring, and is the main venue for the Perth Festival for the Arts. Perth Theatre consists of a proscenium arch theatre and a studio theatre, and is, architecturally, a jewel of a building.

PITLOCHRY FESTIVAL THEATRE
(Pitlochry)

Pitlochry Festival Theatre produces a season of seven plays in repertoire between May and October each year. Situated in the midst of the beautiful surroundings of Pitlochry and the River Tummel, the theatre serves Scots audiences and a mix of tourists, and its playing pattern allows visitors to the theatre to see a number of plays within a period of a few days. The first five plays are brought into the repertoire within the first five weeks of the season and are a mix of Scottish, classic and contemporary, reflecting the different interests of the audience. In addition to the play season, there are regular Sunday night concerts of music, comedy and operetta. Smaller shows are held in the theatre foyer on nights when the theatre is preparing for a main house opening.

ROYAL LYCEUM THEATRE COMPANY (Edinburgh)

The Royal Lyceum Theatre Company in Edinburgh aims to produce theatre of the highest possible quality to excite and stimulate the imagination. The company produces 10 -12 plays each year, from September to April and a summer season of touring and own productions, During August, the theatre is given over to the Edinburgh International Festival. The company presents a programme of contemporary and classical theatre, with a strong and distinctive style. It also runs a year round education programme.

SCOTTISH THEATRE ARCHIVE
(Glasgow)

Housed within the special collections department of Glasgow University Library, the Scottish Theatre Archive is a treasure trove of Scotland's theatrical heritage. Holding scripts, programmes, photographs, press cuttings and production materials as well as some special collections, the archive mounts occasional exhibitions and is open to all those who wish to consult it.

**TRAVERSE THEATRE
(Edinburgh)**

The Traverse Theatre, based in Edinburgh, aims to be Scotland's pre-eminent theatre for new plays. Offering an innovative repertoire of Scottish and international work throughout the year, the Traverse commissions new writers, working with them to produce international premieres. The Traverse runs a writers development programme, including running writers groups, presenting rehearsed readings and hosting public writers workshops. Within the Traverse building, itself of innovative design, the theatre has two auditoria, reflecting the company's ability to present work in a variety of surroundings, and to offer a venue to visiting companies from Britain and abroad. The Traverse also runs an educational programme for schools and youth groups. The Traverse company has toured extensively in Scotland and abroad.

TRON THEATRE (Glasgow)

The Tron Theatre is situated within a converted 18th Century church in the heart of Glasgow, providing atmospheric surroundings for contemporary work. The theatre, seating 272, mainly produces new Scottish drama which is international in terms of its reference and ambition. The Tron presents a year round programme of drama, dance, music and comedy from Scotland, Britain and overseas. The company is particularly interested in developing long term relationships with non UK

presenters and promoters and has toured within the UK, to Canada and to the US.

TOURING COMPANIES

There are also a number of touring companies which are funded on an ongoing revenue basis to provide theatre of quality to a network of theatres, arts centres and community venues across Scotland. These include:

**BORDERLINE THEATRE
COMPANY (Ayr and Scotland)**

Based in Ayr, and with its own theatre facilities, Borderline is a theatre company committed to touring new and contemporary work to a wide cross section of the public. In addition to its work for adult audiences, Borderline has a special concern for children's theatre, and works in schools and community centres to take its work around Scotland.

**COMMUNICADO THEATRE
COMPANY
(Edinburgh and Scotland)**

Communicado tour a minimum of two new plays every year, tackling work which has classic and essentially human themes. Communicado's aim is to create theatre of enormous emotional power. The company's radical style comes from the collaboration of artists with a shared commitment to risk taking and exploration of the whole range of theatre techniques. Unrestricted by accepted rules or theatrical conventions, Communicado regularly alternates from small, scale touring to rural communities, to epic theatre

events in unconventional spaces.

**7:84 THEATRE COMPANY
SCOTLAND
(Glasgow and Scotland)**

7:84 is one of Scotland's leading touring companies, committed to the concept of theatre which engages with the social, cultural and political issues of the day. (The company takes its name from a statistic which indicated that 7% of the population of Britain own 84% of the wealth of the country). The company has a strong commitment to new writing and has performed plays from Ireland, America and Germany in addition to its work commissioned from Scottish writers. 7:84 tours three productions a year and operates an outreach policy, working with people usually denied access to drama.

**TAG THEATRE COMPANY
(Glasgow and Scotland)**

TAG's primary objective is to create high quality contemporary theatre with an associated programme of educational activities which tours to young people across Scotland. In particular, TAG develops theatre experiences which involve collaborations between the medium of drama, dance and music. TAG aims to provide a balanced annual programme of work which achieves the highest artistic and educational standard by: involving young people both as critical spectators and active participators by offering associated educational

programmes of activities including drama and dance workshops, seminars, training and resource material which motivates creative expression accessing the programme of work to the widest audience of young people by touring to schools, colleges, community groups, theatres and arts centres

**WILDCAT STAGE PRODUCTIONS
(Glasgow and Scotland)**

A musical theatre company founded in 1978, Wildcat produces new works by Scottish writers on a large, medium and small scale for touring throughout Britain and abroad. The company produces work for both adult and children's audiences, and has proved particularly popular with an audience brought up on contemporary popular music. The company's work concentrates on the social and political issues of the day as they relate to the lives of ordinary people, and the company has built a popular following amongst people of all ages.

For contact details of the theatres and theatre companies listed above contact:
The Help Desk, The Scottish Arts Council, 12 Manor Place, Edinburgh EH3 7DD
Tel: +44 131 243 2444
Fax: +44 131 477 7241
e-mail:
helpdesk.SAC@artsfb.org.uk

DANCE

Dance is central to the culture of Scotland, and the establishment of the Scottish Traditions of Dance Trust as a focus for research and a contact point for information has been greatly welcomed by all those interested in the history, profile and development of Scotland's traditional dance forms. Elsewhere, the establishment of Dance Productions, the New Moves festival and regional centres of dance in Edinburgh, Glasgow and Aberdeen, is raising the profile of contemporary dance amongst audiences in Scotland. Scotland has only two revenue funded dance companies, one a classical ballet company and the other focusing on contemporary work, but in addition to these companies there are a number of contemporary dance companies funded on a project basis to create work to tour.

DANCE PRODUCTIONS (Edinburgh)

Dance Productions is an independent dance agency which encourages dance promoters through the establishment of a network of dance promoters. Dance Productions encourages dance residencies and provides opportunities for Scottish dancers to work with choreographers with international reputations.

THE SCOTTISH BALLET (Glasgow and Scotland)

The Scottish Ballet is Scotland's only full time classical ballet company. It provides a focus for the art of ballet in Scotland whilst extending the boundaries of the classical style. The company makes accessible to the public the widest range of classical works through a programme of touring classical ballet at large, medium and small scale levels. Scottish Ballet has a full time educational unit and a network of regional dance animateurs. In recent years, the company has toured extensively abroad.

DANCE BASE (Edinburgh)

The regional centre for dance, Dance Base offers a year round programme of dance classes in a range of styles and disciplines for the new dancer through to the seasoned professional. Classes range from flamenco, tap and jazz dance to Indian, Breton and Scottish dance as well as a strong programme of professional contemporary masterclasses and community workshops. Dance Base has a wide range of Scottish based teachers offering a range of classes and also works with visiting professional dancers, choreographers and companies to produce a series of residencies, masterclasses and professional workshops.

SCOTTISH DANCE THEATRE (Dundee and Scotland)

Based in Dundee at the Dundee Rep Theatre, Scottish Dance Theatre is a contemporary dance company of six dancers who produce a repertoire of both established and new pieces of work. The company tours twice a year in Scotland and works with a variety of artists, from choreographers to visual artists and musicians to create the opportunity for experimentation. The company operates an extensive education programme throughout the year. Scottish Dance Theatre is interested in developing links with promoters abroad.

For contact details of the dance organisations listed above contact:
The Help Desk, The Scottish Arts Council, 12 Manor Place, Edinburgh EH3 7DD
Tel: +44 131 243 2444
Fax:+44 131 477 7241
e-mail:
helpdesk.SAC@artsfb.org.uk

PUPPETRY

There are over 30 puppeteers and puppet companies working professionally in Scotland, from the Highlands to the Borders. The following represent only those who have either a building or a resource for puppeteers.

SCOTTISH MASK AND PUPPET CENTRE (Glasgow)

A Glasgow based information centre, the Scottish Mask and Puppet Theatre aims to establish puppet and mask theatre within the mainstream of theatre provision in Scotland. It seeks recognition for puppet theatre as an art form in its own right, and to establish a training provision to advance this aim. The centre is working to maintain and develop a national and international puppet centre, incorporating a museum, an education institute and a modern European scale puppet theatre. The centre has a mask and puppet specialist in residence, an education officer, a special needs puppetry consultant and a film and special effects maker. The centre offers professional performance projects, masterclasses, workshops and courses for adults and children, a reference library and national and international documentation on companies and organisations world-wide. The Scottish Mask and Puppet Centre also houses the Miles Lee Collection of Puppets and Marionettes, and publishes twice yearly a guide to puppeteers across Scotland.

BIGGAR LITTLE THEATRE (Biggar)

The home of the Purves Puppet family, this is a Victorian style family theatre with a unique range of facilities for all types of puppetry, live theatre and miniature concerts. Seating 100, the theatre also houses a puppet museum and presents a programme of puppet shows and workshops when the Purves' company is not on tour.

For contact details of the puppetry organisations listed above contact :
The Help Desk, The Scottish Arts Council, 12 Manor Place, Edinburgh EH3 7DD
Tel: +44 131 243 2444
Fax:+44 131 477 7241
e-mail:
helpdesk.SAC@artsfb.org.uk

VISUAL ART

From contemporary art galleries to sculpture workshops and printmakers' studios, Scotland's visual arts are reflected in a range of work which is displayed in public exhibition spaces throughout the country. In addition to these public spaces, there is also substantial provision for artists workshops and studios.

ABERDEEN ART GALLERY (Aberdeen)

Aberdeen Art Gallery, run by the City of Aberdeen Council, houses one of the most important provincial art collections in the UK and attracts over 350,000 visitors each year.

Built in 1884 to a design in neo-classical style by A Marshall MacKenzie, the Gallery houses works ranging from 18th century portraits by Raeburn, Hogarth, Ramsay and Reynolds to powerful 20th century works by Paul Nash, Ben Nicholson and Francis Bacon. The paintings include excellent examples by Impressionists such as Monet, Pissaro, Sisley and Bonnard and in addition a significant collection of Scottish domestic silver and other decorative arts is normally on show.

The Gallery also presents a lively and diverse series of special exhibitions and events each year, including film, video, literature, music recitals workshops, lectures, dance and drama.

AN LANNTAIR (Stornoway, Isle of Lewis)

One of the most northern galleries in Scotland, An Lanntair uses its Stornoway base to encourage awareness and provide access to all forms of art and, through a bilingual policy, to actively support the Gaelic language through exhibitions and events.

CITY ARTS CENTRE (Edinburgh)

Located next to Waverley Station and originally built as a warehouse in the 1890's, the City Arts Centre has six floors of gallerys pace, served by escalators and a lift. Owned and managed by the City of Edinburgh Council, it is a major temporary exhibition space, with an active and diverse programme showing a wide range of material from contemporary culture to historical antiquities. An important feature of the programme is contemporary art and design; Scottish, British and international. The gallery also houses the City's collection of 19th and 20th Century Scottish art, which is displayed regularly as a series of thematic temporary exhibitions. Admission to the Gallery is free, except for special exhibitions.

2

COLLECTIVE GALLERY (Edinburgh)

An artists based organisation, the Collective Gallery is a forum dedicated to the support and development of emerging contemporary art and artforms. The gallery aims to be a crucial force in the development of emerging artists and to further the critical dialogue within the context of contemporary visual art. Based in Edinburgh, the gallery provides a forum for the exchange of ideas and information, and mounts exhibitions alongside education activities and other events.

EDINBURGH SCULPTURE WORKSHOP (Edinburgh)

Edinburgh Sculpture Workshop encourages the practice of sculpture through education, exhibition and outreach activities. The sculpture workshop offers a fully equipped open workshop for sculptors and artists alongside 12 rented studios. A membership organisation, the Edinburgh sculpture workshop organises education courses, members exhibitions, international artists exchanges and community outreach activities.

THE FRUITMARKET GALLERY (Edinburgh)

Situated in Edinburgh, the Fruitmarket Gallery is committed to showing a progressive and challenging programme of national and international contemporary art, design and architecture. Concerned to bring the best work of leading artists world-wide to Scotland and to exhibit the work of Scottish artists in an international context, engaging with contemporary issues, the Fruitmarket Gallery stages 7 to 8 contemporary exhibitions per year for public access. The gallery runs an extensive education and events programme and has a well stocked bookshop with a changing stock of titles covering all areas of contemporary art, art practice and theory.

GLASGOW MUSEUMS AND GALLERIES (Glasgow)

The City of Glasgow Council is fortunate in having some of Scotland's most impressive museums and galleries. The Burrell Collection, in Pollok Park houses the collection of Sir William Burrell, a Glasgow entrepreneur who travelled the world collecting treasures from paintings to furniture and glassware which are now housed in a purpose built gallery. Temporary exhibitions are also staged within the Burrell.

In March 1996, Glasgow opened the Gallery of Modern Art, converted from a former mansion built in 1778, and until recently used as a library. Refurbished at a cost of over £7 million, this spectacular gallery comprises four floors with over 24,000 square feet of display space as well as the temporary exhibitions space, a shop and a roof top cafe. This new gallery features contemporary paintings and sculptures by living artists. The gallery houses work by Scottish artists including John Bellany, Alison Watt and Ken Currie as well as the work of British artists like David Hockney, Paula Rego, Alan Davie and David Kemp. The work of international artists of the calibre of Niki de Saint Phalle and Sebastiao Salgado is also displayed in the four galleries named after four elements: Earth, Fire, Water and Air.

Kelvingrove Art Gallery and Museum, The People's Palace, St. Mungo Museum of Religious Life and Art, Provand's Lordship and Pollok House also house many interesting collections ranging from armour, costume, ancient artefacts and displays of working class Glaswegian life through to religious art at the various venues which comprise the City of Glasgow's Art Galleries and Museums.

GLASGOW SCULPTURE STUDIOS (Glasgow)

Glasgow Sculpture Studios were founded by a group of art school graduates in 1988. They are based in a converted warehouse in Maryhill, a working class area north of the city centre. The studios are large and well equipped and provide permanent studio spaces for twenty six artists. The studio has approximately 150 artists in membership, most of whom use the workshops on a short term basis throughout the year.

Glasgow Sculpture Studios are planning a major expansion in 1997, with funding from the National Lottery. This will include extra studio spaces to cope with demand, improved workshop equipment, a range of new facilities, and a substantial public area dedicated to an educational programme and containing an exhibition space. The larger premises will also provide studios reserved for visiting artists, especially from abroad. The development of international links is a particular priority of the studios, and individual artists frequently travel within Europe. New links with North America are currently being developed.

McMANUS GALLERIES (Dundee)

Built in 1867 and designed by Sir George Gilbert Scott, the McManus Galleries are owned and run by Dundee City Council and house an art collection of national importance. The collections include fine examples of 19th and 20th Century Scottish paintings, prints, drawings, sculpture, furniture, clocks, glass, ceramics and silver. The McManus Galleries also house Dundee's human history collections. Three galleries tell the story of the region from prehistoric times through the Industrial Revolution and into the 20th Century. The costume gallery looks at clothes and customs with thematic displays, and the Archaeological Gallery has a significant display of material from Ancient Egypt. There is a programme of changing exhibitions alongside more permanent displays using the collections.

PIER ARTS CENTRE (Stromness, Isle of Orkney)

On the island of Orkney, the Pier Arts Centre in Stromness presents contemporary art produced on the island, and brings to Orkney significant art from Scotland, the UK and beyond. The gallery preserves and presents an important collection of 20th Century art.

PORTFOLIO GALLERY (Edinburgh)

The Portfolio Gallery's policy is the promotion of photography as an art form, to a broad audience, through exhibition, education and publishing. The gallery presents an international programme of contemporary photographic exhibitions with particular emphasis on the work of British based photographic artists, and commissions and tours new photographic work both nationally and internationally. The gallery also publishes PORTFOLIO - The Catalogue of Contemporary British Photography, the UK's leading photography journal, which involves the commissioning of essays, the publishing of portfolios of new work and critical reviews of exhibitions.

SCOTTISH SCULPTURE WORKSHOPS (Lumsden, Aberdeen)

Founded in 1979 in Lumsden, Aberdeenshire, the Scottish Sculpture Workshop is the most important venue for artists visiting the UK to make sculpture - 50% of all overseas artists who come to the UK to make work use the workshop facilities of self-catering accommodation, as well as facilities to make work in wood, steel, iron, ceramic, stone (including granite), cast bronze and aluminium. Located in the foothills of the Highlands in countryside characterised by ancient standing stones, medieval castles and whisky distilleries, a visit to the Scottish Sculpture Workshop offers the artists an opportunity to concentrate on work in peaceful surroundings, to explore new media and to meet a wide range of Scottish, British and overseas artists.

STILLS (Edinburgh)

Stills Gallery promotes and develops the work of Scottish contemporary photographic artists, and seeks to increase the standard and diversity of photography exhibited in Scotland. Staging a minimum of 8 photography exhibitions by Scottish and international photographers and education events including artists' talks, workshops and seminars, the gallery aims to have digital and conventional dark rooms installed by mid 1996.

STREET LEVEL GALLERY (Glasgow)

Street Level is a photographic gallery and workshop which aims to foster an active and dynamic photographic culture in Glasgow by stimulating an interest in the practice and appreciation of photography. Street Level organises an annual programme of exhibitions, promotes access through its education programme and provides training in various photographic techniques. The gallery provides consultancy for organisations setting up photographic projects and workshops. A number of Street Level exhibitions tour to other venues in Britain and abroad.

THE TALBOT RICE GALLERY (Edinburgh)

Housed in the heart of Edinburgh University, the Talbot Rice Gallery houses a permanent collection of artworks and promotes links with the community by showing temporary exhibitions of varied contemporary art, supported by a wide range of interpretative material. The gallery specialises in exhibiting the work of mid-career artists from Scotland and elsewhere.

TRANSMISSION GALLERY (Glasgow)

Established in 1983, Transmission is a Glasgow based artspace administered on a voluntary basis by a committee of practising artworkers. Transmission has a membership of over 200, many of whom are local artists and who are encouraged to initiate projects and proposals, both within the gallery itself and elsewhere in the city. Transmission develops contact and long term links with other artist-run spaces and organisations. This includes the promotion of an international exchange programme which has included Arnhem, Bergen, Flanders, Belfast, Chicago and Cologne. Transmission presents a platform for experimental/ time based work, including film, video installation, performance, live music and sound events as well as supporting the work of less established artists and aiding the distribution of small press and, artist produced magazines and books.

WORKSHOPS AND ARTISTS STUDIO SPACES (Glasgow and Scotland)

WASPS is an artists organisation which provides high quality, low cost studios combined with a pro-active and responsive property management service to around 500 fine and applied artists at 11 locations throughout Scotland. WASPS works with local authorities' development agencies to identify suitable buildings for visual arts use, and promotes the development of studio facilities to as many communities throughout Scotland as possible, as well as participating in and initiating international artists exchanges.

PRINTMAKERS

There are a variety of Printmaking Galleries and Workshops throughout Scotland, each offering printmaking facilities for artists from Scotland and beyond. Facilities on offer range from stone and plate lithography, etching, screen printing and relief printing. Many printmakers workshops have their own gallery spaces in which temporary exhibitions are mounted and run open access classes, courses and demonstrations. There are Printmakers Workshops in Aberdeen, at Peacock Printmakers; in Dundee at the Seagate Gallery; in Edinburgh, at Edinburgh Printmakers Workshop; in Glasgow, at Glasgow Print Studio and in Inverness, at Highland Printmakers Workshop and Galleries.

For contact details of the visual arts organisations listed above contact:
The Help Desk, The Scottish Arts Council, 12 Manor Place, Edinburgh EH3 7DD
Tel: +44 131 243 2444
Fax:+44 131 477 7241
e-mail:
helpdesk.SAC@artsfb.org.uk

LITERATURE

Scotland is rightly proud of its literary heritage, from Walter Scott to Robert Burns and Robert Louis Stevenson through to contemporary Scottish writers such as James Kelman, Janice Galloway, A.L. Kennedy and William McIlvanney and poets such as Sorley Maclean, Ian Crichton Smith, Liz Lochhead and Robert Crawford. A number of organisations exist which help to promote literature in Scotland. Those marked with an asterisk* can be found in one location, at the Scottish Book Centre, 137 Dundee Street, Edinburgh.

ASSOCIATION FOR SCOTTISH LITERARY STUDIES (Aberdeen and Scotland)

The Association for Scottish Literary Studies exists to promote the study, teaching and writing of Scottish literature and to promote the languages of Scotland. The association stimulates and co-ordinates the publication and editing of works of Scottish literature and publishes edited texts, reprints, scholarly studies and periodicals. The association maintains a continuous programme of publications and conferences.

BOOK TRUST SCOTLAND (Edinburgh and Scotland)

Book Trust Scotland works with teachers, writers, librarians, illustrators and enthusiasts to promote reading and, in particular Scottish books, amongst people throughout Scotland. The Book Trust offers an information service and administers the Kathleen Fidler Award for a first novel for children, and the McVitie's Prize for the Scottish Writer of the Year. The trust also runs campaigns to promote readership amongst people of all ages, including the "Now Read On" campaign, and operates a children's reference library.*

SCOTTISH PUBLISHERS ASSOCIATION (Edinburgh and Scotland)

The Scottish Publishers Association aims to help publishing concerns in Scotland to conduct their book publishing business in a professional manner, to market their output to the widest possible readership within Scotland, the UK and overseas and to encourage the development of a literary culture in Scotland. The Association offers a free quarterly newsletter with marketing, trade fair, employment, overseas and general publishing information and information, advice and access to the Association's reference and resource library. Amongst a wide range of services offered, the Association offers representation at book fairs at home and abroad and a comprehensive training programme.*

SCOTTISH POETRY LIBRARY
(Edinburgh and Scotland)

The Scottish Poetry Library seeks to make visible and accessible to the public the poetry of Scotland in whatever language it is written, and to provide a selection of mainly modern poetry from other countries. The Library seeks to enhance the status of poetry and its acceptance amongst the practised arts through the provision of an information and resource centre for poetry, through a computerised database, audio and videotape, backed up by catalogues and thus to encourage increased study and awareness of Scots poets and poetry, within Scotland and abroad. The Library promotes and encourages poetry's links with other art forms and also international contacts through residencies, and translations from, as well as into, Scotland's languages. The Library publishes a quarterly newsletter.

For contact details of the literature organisations listed above contact:
The Help Desk, The Scottish Arts Council, 12 Manor Place, Edinburgh EH3 7DD
Tel: +44 131 243 2444
Fax:+44 131 477 7241
e-mail:
helpdesk.SAC@artsfb.org.uk

ARTS CENTRES

In addition to venues and events dedicated to specific art forms, Scotland has a network of arts centres and associations which aims to provide access to a wide range of art forms, serving a geographical area.

CENTRE FOR CONTEMPORARY ARTS (Glasgow)

The Centre for Contemporary Arts (CCA) is one of the UK's premier venues for new art. The Centre supports artists in making possible the creation of original work and aims to increase the accessibility and strengthen the understanding of contemporary arts through a broad range of activities. The Centre houses two gallery spaces, two performance spaces, an award winning cafe bar and a specialist arts bookshop. CCA offers an innovative and varied programme of exhibitions, performance, writers' events, talks, tours, classes and workshops by artists from abroad.

CRAWFORD ARTS CENTRE
(St Andrews)

From a rural base in the university town of St Andrews, the Crawford Centre aims to present the highest quality arts activities to the public, maintaining its position as a centre for the arts activities in Fife, with a significance extending to the rest of Scotland and beyond. The Crawford Centre offers a programme of temporary visual arts and crafts exhibitions, an artists studio for residencies and fellowships, art classes and talks for adults and art workshops for young people. The centre has a studio theatre for hire to amateur and professional groups and manages, in association with the Byre Theatre, the St. Andrews Youth Theatre.

EDEN COURT THEATRE
(Inverness)

Eden Court Theatre is the largest cultural centre for the Highlands and Islands. Serving an area equivalent to the size of Belgium, Eden Court is a touring venue for large scale theatrical, musical, operatic and dance productions. The venue also houses a cinema and promotes rock concerts and conferences. Eden Court Theatre has a team of outreach workers comprising an Education Officer, a Drama Artist in Residence and a Film Officer.

THE LEMON TREE
(Aberdeen)

The Lemon Tree has two performance spaces, a cafe theatre and a studio theatre. It seeks to promote an exciting and diverse range of events and activities for the entire community in a friendly and welcoming manner, and to create opportunities and provide support which enables and encourages artists to realise their full potential. The Lemon Tree promotes a wide ranging programme of live arts events, music, comedy, theatre and dance, seven days a week. The theatre programme is biased towards physical theatre, new writing and unconventional contemporary adaptations of classic work.

The dance programme includes contemporary, jazz and non-western dance forms. Musically, the centre offers a widely varied programme from traditional to Cajun, bluegrass, rock and indie. There is also an informal exhibition space featuring the work of local and regionally based artists.

LYTH ARTS CENTRE
(Lyth, Caithness)

Lyth Arts Centre is a small scale venue near John O' Groats in the far north of Scotland. Founded in 1977, Lyth Arts Centre's programme is devoted to presenting professional artists and performers from other parts of the country, but the centre also acts as a stepping off point for local artistic endeavour.

The centre presents programmes of contemporary theatre, music and dance - often innovative and experimental. Performances are staged between April and September and companies give one or two performances which are sometimes linked to workshop sessions in local schools. Companies are occasionally invited to undertake short residencies while preparing new work.

Each year, the centre presents one exhibition programme of contemporary fine art which is set up in late June and runs daily through-out July and August.

MACROBERT ARTS CENTRE
(Stirling)

The MacRobert Arts Centre presents a year round mixed programme of all artforms from drama and visual art to contemporary dance, crafts and jazz. The MacRobert is also a regional film theatre screening a varied programme of film. The Centre has a five hundred seat theatre, a 149 seat studio theatre, a foyer area used for informal concerts and a gallery. An arts team of Film Development Officer, Drama Artist in Residence and resident young people's theatre company, Visible Fictions, work with many schools and community groups.

THEATRE WORKSHOP
(Edinburgh)

Theatre Workshop aims to provide access to the arts as a means of expression for the widest number of people, particularly those that are, in some way, disadvantaged by their place in society. In assessing priorities, Theatre Workshop gives priority to people with special needs; minority ethnic communities; women; children and young people and disadvantaged communities.

Through their work, Theatre Workshop seeks to pursue a progressive, high quality educational programme in a broad range of theatre activities and to be a resource for community development through setting the work in the context of social and cultural change.

LANGUAGE

Scotland is a country of many languages and dialects, some indigenous, some brought to Scotland by travellers who have subsequently made Scotland their home. The culture of Scotland is enriched by all of these, and there are a number of artists and organisations who seek to promote these languages and cultures throughout Scotland. From the Edinburgh Chinese Dance and Cultural Group, the Mauritian Cultural Association and the Indian Arts Council to the Asian Cultural Association, the Pakistan Art and Literary Circle to the Music Village and the Bangla Centre, there are multi-cultural arts activities throughout Scotland. These are just a few:

AN COMUNN GAIDHEALACH
(Stornoway and Scotland)

An Comunn Gaidhealach seeks to develop and promote Gaelic nationally as a living language by encouraging the study of Gaelic literature, music, drama, arts and crafts. In the pursuance of this end, An Comunn organises and stages the Royal National Mod, a major Gaelic language arts festival held in a different part of Scotland in October of each year. An Comunn branches also organises around 20 local mods, ceilidhs and festivals throughout Scotland.

COMHAIRLE NAN LEABHRAICHEAN
(Glasgow and Scotland)

The Gaelic Books Council provides publication grants for individual Gaelic books as well as commissioning authors and selling books direct to the public by post and through bookstalls at specific events. Comhairle nan Leabhraichean publicises Gaelic books in print through its catalogue, Leabhraichean Gaidhlig, and offers an editorial and word processing service. The Gaelic Books Council welcomes queries and publishes an annual report which is free of charge on request.

FEISAN NAN GAIDHEAL
(Skye and Scotland)

The Gaelic word Feis (plural Feisan) simply means a festival, but in the past few years has become particularly associated with tuition based festivals. Feisan are generally organised by community based voluntary organisations, where people over a wide age range, but primarily young people, are offered training in skills in the Gaelic language and its associated traditional music, song and dance. Throughout Scotland, the Feis movement has grown in the past eleven years from the first Feis in Barra in 1981, to 29 Feisan (25 of them tuition based) throughout Scotland.

Feisan Nan Gaidheal is the National Association of Gaelic Arts Festivals, wholly owned and run by the community Feisan throughout the country to provide support, lobbying, co-ordination, links with other bodies, assistance with development, training of a high standard, promotion and tuition materials and to identify new resources.

MELA
(Glasgow and Edinburgh)

The Mela are Asian cultural festivals, with music and dance from India, Pakistan, Bangladesh, China, Sri Lanka, Indonesia, Singapore and Switzerland. The Mela offer, in addition to performances, exhibitions, stalls, street performances and different types of food from the various nations represented.

NATIONAL GAELIC ARTS PROJECT
(Stornoway and Scotland)

The National Gaelic Arts Project is the arts wing of Comunn Na Gaidhlig, the principal Gaelic language development organisation. It has as its principal aim the co-ordination, development and promotion of the Gaelic arts, including traditional and contemporary artforms, film and television. The project offers arts and media training through an extensive programme of short courses and workshops. It produces touring theatre, exhibitions and music events for both live and televised performance, and is working towards the development of a Gaelic cultural infrastructure through the foundation of a theatre company, an art gallery, a TV service, teaching festivals and a comprehensive database and archive.

TOSG (Skye and Scotland)
Scotland's Gaelic language theatre company launched in 1996 tours two projects annually from its base at Sabhal Mor Ostaig, the Gaelic College on the island of Skye. Tosg works throughout Scotland and undertakes an extensive education programme, working with young and older Gaelic speakers.

For contact details of the Gaelic and multi-cultural arts organisations listed above contact:
The Help Desk, The Scottish Arts Council, 12 Manor Place, Edinburgh EH3 7DD
Tel: +44 131 243 2444
Fax: +44 131 477 7241
e-mail:
helpdesk.SAC@artsfb.org.uk

ARTS DEVELOPMENT

All arts organisations are encouraged to offer a proactive education programme and to devise policies which will ensure access and choice to all those who wish to make use of the arts, but some organisations have been established specifically to consider these areas.

ARTLINK
(Edinburgh and Lothians)
Artlink believes that participation in the arts is a right and promotes equal access to the arts and opportunity for people with experience of disability to participate in the arts, whether actively or passively. Artlink's escort service enables attendance at arts events; its arts programmes

work with users and in collaboration with other organisations to establish a network of opportunities for learning and practical activity in all forms of the creative arts.

ART IN PARTNERSHIP
(Edinburgh and Scotland)
Art In Partnership provides a full project management and commissioning service aimed at creating a greater awareness and understanding of art outside the Gallery context. Established in 1985, Art In Partnership is the leading public art agency in Scotland. A team of five visual art specialists work with a broad range of clients to develop public art programmes which put Scotland at the forefront of contemporary art practice within Europe.

The agency aims to foster new collaborations with artists, engineers, architects, environmentalists and design professionals. Clients from the public and private sectors are encouraged to explore the parameters of a project at the earliest stages. Liaison between the artist, client the design team and the user groups is perceived as a vital part of maximising the strategic benefits of each initiative.

Scope and scale of projects vary from the large and long term M8 project involving a number of artists and organisations to a series of site specific commissions - reception desk, tapestry, tiled floor design and glass panels for the new Scottish Office building in Edinburgh.

DUMFRIES AND GALLOWAY ARTS ASSOCIATION
(Dumfries and Galloway)
Dumfries and Galloway Arts Association increases access to the arts for all in the south west of Scotland. Through the promotion of arts events, artists' residencies covering visual art, writers, music and dance and by developing specific events such as professional productions and community collaborations, the association assists in ensuring that the arts are available to all in a geographically disparate, rural community.

HEALTH CARE ARTS
(Dundee and Scotland)
Health Care Arts is a Scotland wide organisation for the development of the visual arts and crafts in healthcare facilities. Its philosophy revolves around three key ideas: that all art in a healthcare setting should be of the highest quality of skill and imagination; that it should be appropriate to its site and audience and that it should celebrate the locality.

Healthcare Arts seeks to extend and develop innovative and effective applications for the work of visual artists and craftspeople in creating environments conducive to healing and a quality of life for those in health institutions which assists the delivery of care. Its work in the planning and managing of commissions of art and craft works within the upgrading of existing buildings or construction of new buildings continues to expand, alongside work with an artists residency programme

in a mental health hospital and the expansion of a crafts residency post. The cultivation of its work with hospices continues to thrive.

Healthcare Arts has published a full colour guide to crafts in healthcare which promotes good practice, and has co-ordinated the production of a further guide for the visual arts.

PROJECT ABILITY (Glasgow)
Project Ability aims to make the arts accessible to all people in the community and to support and encourage the artistic abilities of people of all ages whose opportunities have been limited by disability, ill health or poverty. Project Ability works in particular with young people and adults with a learning disability, with a physical disability, with an experience of mental illness and with older people. The company supports disabled people in promoting their work through the staging of exhibitions and other public events. It works in partnership with care providers in social work, education, health care and the voluntary sector.

SHETLAND ARTS TRUST
(Lerwick, Isle of Shetland)
Set up in Lerwick in 1985 to promote, co-ordinate and develop the arts in Shetland, the Trust undertakes a wide range of arts initiatives. The Shetland Arts Trust supports approximately 50 local arts initiatives in addition to undertaking its own promotions. Shetland Arts Trust also owns and manages the Weisdale Mill, a small art

gallery and textile museum for the presentation of local and touring exhibition.

For contact details of the arts development organisations listed above contact:
The Help Desk, The Scottish Arts Council, 12 Manor Place, Edinburgh EH3 7DD
Tel: +44 131 243 2444
Fax:+44 131 477 7241
e-mail:
helpdesk.SAC@artsfb.org.uk

TRAMWAY (Glasgow)

A former Tram depot, owned and operated by the Performing Arts Department of Glasgow City Council, Tramway is one of the UK's most celebrated "found spaces". The building was given a new lease of life in 1988 when Peter Brook brought his celebrated production of the Mahabarata to Glasgow. Now firmly established as one of Europe's most prestigious multi-purpose performance and exhibition spaces, with an emphasis on the contemporary and the cutting edge, Tramway provides both a showcase for international work and a focus for young Scottish art.

For contact details of the arts centres listed above contact:
The Help Desk, The Scottish Arts Council, 12 Manor Place, Edinburgh EH3 7DD
Tel: +44 131 243 2444
Fax:+44 131 477 7241
e-mail:
helpdesk.SAC@artsfb.org.uk

FILM ORGANISATIONS IN SCOTLAND

SCOTTISH SCREEN LOCATIONS

Scotland's National Film Commission was established in 1990 to market Scotland as a base for location filming and to promote the local industry services and infrastructure. Based in Edinburgh, Scottish Screen Locations offers a completely free service to film-makers with a single door approach to location shooting in Scotland. With an extensive photolibrary and database of locations, facilities and local contacts, the organisation will advise on all aspects of a Scottish shoot, providing location research and helping with initial reconnoitring. Scottish Screen Locations has been used to assist with productions such as Rob Roy, Braveheart, Highlander III and The Glace Bay Miners Museum.

SCOTTISH FILM PRODUCTION FUND

The Scottish Film Production Fund was established in 1982 to nurture and support Scottish film making. It receives grant aid from the Scottish Office Education and Industry Department and also from Channel 4, BBC Scotland and Grampian Television. The Fund provides financial assistance to independent producers for the development of feature films - research, scriptwriting, budgeting, location research and casting. Initial support does not usually exceed £15,000 though further help may be available to bring the project to the point where full production finance can be found. The SFPF does not contribute to feature film production finance, but has recently helped develop movies such as Rob Roy, Shallow Grave and Small Faces. The Fund runs short film schemes: Tartan Shorts, Prime Cuts and the Gaelic Language Geur Ghearr. The Oscar winning 'Franz Kafka's It's a Wonderful Life' is a Tartan Short.

The SFPF also administers the Glasgow Film Fund which it helped to establish with the assistance of the Glasgow Development Agency, Glasgow City Council, the European Regional Development Fund and the Strathclyde European Partnership. This fund offers production finance to either Glasgow based production companies or to projects shooting in the Glasgow area. The Scottish Film Production Fund is actively seeking to create a pan-Scottish film fund bringing in the local enterprise companies and is also exploring ways of raising private finance for film production. The SFPF works with the Scottish Arts Council, advising its National Lottery Committee on applications for film funding.

2

SCOTTISH BROADCAST AND FILM TRAINING

Scottish Broadcast and Film Training is a non profit making agency whose mission is to develop a talented and skilled workforce that will sustain and advance the broadcast film and video industries in Scotland. The organisation is a partnership of Scottish Television, BBC Scotland, the Scottish Film Council, Grampian TV, the Producers Alliance for Cinema and Television, Border TV, the Federation of Entertainment Unions and the Gaelic Television Committee. The company organises and co-ordinates high quality training in response to the industry's specific needs. Schemes include training for new entrants and practical training in editing, researching and the application of new technologies. The aim is to keep Scotland at the leading edge of all aspects of production. Scottish Broadcast and Film Training also administers the Glasgow Producers Development Initiative and the Glasgow Television Development Fund.

EDINBURGH AND LOTHIAN SCREEN INDUSTRIES OFFICE

Established in 1990, the Screen Industries Office is a local film commission, acting as a contact point for productions coming into the area and providing a free liaison service. The Screen Industries Office gives location advice and information on crews, facilities and services. It also administers the Edinburgh Development Fund, providing finance to help develop incoming film and TV projects.

1 'Claustrophobia', The Maly Drama Theatre of St. Petersburgh, Tramway   2 'Sugar Hiccup', Elisabeth Ballet, Tramway   3 (overleaf) 'Taggart', Scottish Television

The Edinburgh Producers Development Initiative is a source of funding for local producers needing to access training, international marketing and distribution opportunities.

COMATAIDH TELEBHISEIN GAIDHLIG

The Gaelic Television Committee (CTG) was established under the 1990 Broadcasting Act to administer the Gaelic Television Fund. The CTG launched its programme service in January 1993. It is funded by The Scottish Office and regulated by the Independent Television Commission.

The CTG has a remit to promote Gaelic as a living language through the funding of a wide range of Gaelic television programmes (up to 200 hours per annum): financing the training of personnel involved in the making of such programmes and financing the undertaking of audience research amongst the Gaelic speaking community.

For further information about film organisations in Scotland contact:
The Scottish Film Council,
74 Victoria Crescent Road,
Glasgow G12 9JN
Tel: +44 141 334 4445
Fax:+44 141 334 8132
e-mail
SFC@cityscape.co.uk

TRADE UNIONS

The arts in Scotland, as elsewhere in the world, are able to flourish only as a result of the efforts of the thousands of cultural workers whose work is often poorly rewarded on a financial level. In order to achieve some reasonable terms and conditions of employment, artists are represented by trade unions, who negotiate minimum terms and conditions of employment with the appropriate employers associations. These are the main unions in the industry.

SCOTTISH TRADES UNION CONGRESS
(Glasgow and Scotland)

The Scottish Trades Union Congress is an independent, autonomous organisation and is the only trade union centre in Scotland. All trade unions with a membership in Scotland are affiliated to the STUC. The principle purpose of the STUC is to act as a focus for the collective work of trade unions in bettering the working and living conditions of trade union members in Scotland. To achieve this aim, the STUC has a number of different committees, including education and training, health and social services, housing and local government and arts, media and culture. The arts, media and culture committee is serviced by the Arts Officer of the STUC, a full time post. The Arts Officer has the remit of increasing access to the arts by trade union members and their families, and of furthering co-operation between trade unions and arts organisations.

The Arts Officer also develops policy and campaigns on cultural matters for the STUC to promote to trade unions, arts bodies and Government at European, national and local level.

BRITISH ACTORS EQUITY ASSOCIATION
(Glasgow and Scotland)

Responsible for the terms and conditions of employment of professional actors, singers, stage management, variety artists, directors and designers in the theatre and in television, Equity has a Scottish membership of 2,000. Over the last twenty years, Equity has argued for the development and use of Scottish based talent throughout Scotland's theatre and television industries.

BROADCASTING, ENTERTAINMENT CINEMATOGRAPH AND THEATRE UNION
(Glasgow and Scotland)

BECTU is the trade union responsible for stage and television technicians, camera operators and other craft workers in the film, theatre and television sector. BECTU also has a visual artists section which individual artists can join and represents many administration staff in theatres.

MUSICIANS UNION
(Glasgow and Scotland)

The Musicians' Union represents musicians of all types, whether in the orchestra pit or on the stage. From traditional and jazz bands and band singers to classical musicians, the Musicians' Union offers a union training service for musicians wishing to learn more about the management of the music business, and an instrument insurance scheme.

For enquiries about arts unions in Scotland, contact:
The Arts Officer, the Scottish Trades Union Congress,
16 Woodlands Terrace,
Glasgow G3 6DF
Tel: +44 141 332 4946
Fax:+44 141 332 4649